AF700665

New York Civil Practice

Jeffrey A. Helewitz, JD, LLM, MBA

Copyright © 2000
All rights reserved.
Pearson Publications Company
Dallas, Texas

Website: Pearsonpub-legal.com

ISBN 0-929563-58-1

ACKNOWLEDGMENTS

The author wishes to acknowledge the invaluable assistance of the following persons: the excruciatingly grammatical and breathtakingly brilliant Leak K. Edwards and the naturally litigious and painstakingly particular Daniel Alter. Any and all correct statements appearing in this text are due to their diligence.

Jeffrey A. Helewitz, JD, LLM, MBA

The publisher also thanks Lance A. Cooper, Esq., for his superb editorial contribution.

Enika P. Schulze, Publisher

TABLE OF CONTENTS

Chapter One
Overview of Civil Litigation

Chapter Two
Commencement of a Civil Action

Chapter Three
Pleadings

Chapter Four
Motion Practice

Chapter Five
Discovery

Chapter Six
Trial

Chapter Seven
Judgments and Appeals

Chapter Eight
Other Proceedings

OVERVIEW OF CIVIL LITIGATION

Introduction

The term "civil litigation" denotes the process and procedure necessary to adjudicate a dispute between two individuals, arising from a private injury. This definition contrasts civil litigation from criminal litigation, in which the injured party is society at large whose interests are represented by the government.

In New York, the rules and regulations governing civil disputes are contained in the **New York Civil Practice Law and Rules** (hereinafter referred to as the **CPLR**). These statutes establish all of the regulations and requirements for litigating a civil matter in the New York state court system. If the dispute is one that can or must be adjudicated in one of the federal courts that sits in New York, the governing statutes are the Federal Rules of Civil Procedure (litigation in the federal courts in New York is discussed in Chapter Eight). However, the main purpose of this text is to familiarize the paralegal with the civil procedural rules governing state court actions.

The Role of the Paralegal

Civil litigation remains the area of the law that employs the greatest number of paralegals. The paralegal is crucial to the efficient and effective case management of a problem through the New York court system. In assisting the attorney in the litigation of a civil dispute, paralegals are called upon to provide the following services:

- *Document Management*. The paralegal is responsible for keeping track of all documents that either arrive at or are sent from the law office with respect to a particular case. To accomplish this task the paralegal typically creates an **index file** in which all documents are listed, categorized, and traced so that the placement and state of any document can be readily ascertained.

- *Information Organization*. The paralegal usually is the first person to acquire information from the client; obtain police, accident, and medical reports; locate experts; and organize the gathered information into a logical format to aid in the preparation of materials to be available for the court and in the preparation of the trial.
- *Maintain the Calendar*. As will be discussed throughout the text, the legal process imposes strict time controls as to when documents must be filed with the court or served on parties to the lawsuit. The paralegal, in many instances, is responsible for maintaining a calendar so that the law office can meet these statutory time requirements.
- *Legal Research*. The paralegal may be asked to research the applicable law, both statutory and common. The attorney will use this information to convince the court of the correctness of the client's position and to prepare the evidence necessary to maintain that particular kind of lawsuit.
- *Gather Facts*. In addition to determining the applicable law, the paralegal is required to gather relevant facts that pertain to the lawsuit. This may involve interviewing the client, prospective witnesses, expert witnesses, and obtaining physical evidence that pertains to the matter at hand.
- *Prepare Pleadings*. The paralegal is usually responsible for preparing the initial drafts of pleadings that must be filed with the court. The term **pleadings** describes all documents that are filed incident to a lawsuit. The specific pleadings will be discussed in detail throughout the text.
- *Acquire Authorizations*. One of the paralegal's information-gathering tasks is to prepare authorizations for the client's signature so that medical, employment, tax, and other records

that are deemed confidential or privileged and are not under the client's control can be obtained.

- *Determining Proof of Facts*. The paralegal will aid the attorney in deciding and determining which facts must be proved to the court according to the dictates of the substantive law.
- *Trial Assistance*. The paralegal will accompany the attorney to the trial and typically is responsible for maintaining control over all documents and physical evidence that the attorney will need during the course of the litigation. The paralegal is also involved in general trial preparation, such as preparing the client and witnesses immediately before trial.
- *Posttrial Process*. The paralegal assists in all posttrial activities, including execution against property to satisfy the claim and any appeal of the trial court's verdict.

As can be seen, the role of the paralegal with respect to civil litigation is both challenging and varied.

Evolution of a Civil Dispute

Civil litigation can take place only if a person has been legally injured in some way. This means that an individual has failed to meet a legal duty he or she owes to another, and this failure has resulted in some legal harm to the other person. The basis of every civil lawsuit must be a legal wrong that can only be redressed by the involvement of the court. The legal injury that the person suffers must be an injury that is recognized either by the common law or by statute. This legal injury gives rise to the grounds for instituting the civil lawsuit.

Example: A woman is crossing the street when a car runs a light and hits her. As a result of this incident, the woman breaks her leg and three ribs, needs medical attention, and cannot work for a period of time. The driver of the motor vehicle has breached a duty imposed by law—not to run a red light—and has caused an injury; therefore, the woman may sue the driver for the injuries she has suffered.

Example: *A woman attends a charity dance where a socially prominent dowager whom she has been eager to meet snubs her. The woman feels hurt and depressed, but she has suffered no legal injury that can be redressed by the court. The dowager is under no legal duty to be friendly to strangers.*

Once a legal injury has occurred, the injured party is responsible for bringing the injury to the attention of the court by filing a document known as a **complaint**. To institute a civil action, the injured party must file the complaint with the appropriate court, (i.e., a court that has the authority to hear the matter and that can impose its orders on the alleged wrongdoer). As will be discussed below, a court may only hear matters that fall within the authority of that particular court, and further may only adjudicate conflicts involving persons over whom the court has authority to enforce rulings.

When the complaint has been filed, the injured party, now known as the **plaintiff**, is required to notify the alleged wrongdoer, now known as the **defendant**, that a lawsuit has been instituted against him or her. Failure to notify the defendant of the lawsuit in an appropriate manner will result in the dismissal of the suit.

Example: *A plaintiff has filed a complaint with the court and attempts to notify the defendant of the lawsuit by placing a notice in an envelope addressed to the defendant and then throwing the envelope in the sewer in the belief that eventually it will find its way to the defendant's house. This "sewer service" (once a very prevalent practice in New York) is now deemed totally ineffective as a method of notifying the defendant of the pending litigation.*

Once notified, the defendant has the right to challenge the validity of the lawsuit, either by filing a motion or an answer. A **motion** is a request made to the court asking the court to take a particular action. An **answer** is a formal document used by defendants to respond to the allegations of wrongdoing listed in the plaintiff's complaint.

<u>Example</u>: *The woman from the previous example sues the dowager claiming that the dowager's failure to talk to her has caused her extreme emotional distress. The dowager files a motion with the court to dismiss the action because the woman has failed to state a legal cause of action.*

<u>Example</u>: *The woman from the first example sues the driver of the motor vehicle who hit her. The driver files an answer with the court in which he claims that he did not run the light, the light was green, and it was the plaintiff who caused the accident by jumping into the street against the light.*

If the defendant answers the complaint, the plaintiff has the right to reply to the answer; then, after any reply is made, the discovery process begins. **Discovery** refers to the process of ascertaining all material facts that pertain to the lawsuit. New York requires the parties to attempt to resolve as many issues as possible before the trial and, to this end, permits the litigants to seek information from each other in order to defend against or prove the allegations.

If the parties cannot reach a compromise after discovery is completed, the court will set a trial date at which time the parties will have their dispute resolved either by a judge or a jury. The trial court is responsible for determining the facts of the case; the judge then applies the law to the facts as proven to grant or deny relief to the plaintiff.

At the conclusion of the trial, the losing party may seek a review of the proceeding, either by requesting the judge to reconsider by filing an appropriate motion or by appealing that trial court's decision to a court with authority to review the decisions of the trial court.

<u>Example</u>: *A plaintiff loses a lawsuit because of what she believes to be a misapplication of the law to the facts she proved. The judge denies her motion to reconsider, and so she files an appeal to the court with authority to review the decision of the trial court to determine whether the trial court correctly applied the law to the facts.*

The New York court structure provides for a two-tiered appellate review process so that the unsuccessful litigant may have the opportunity to have the trial court's decision reviewed by two appellate tribunals. This corresponds to the federal court system, which also provides for two levels of appeal. Once all opportunities for appeal have been exhausted, the case is deemed to be finally and conclusively adjudicated.

The New York Court Structure

The structure of the New York court system derives from Article VI of the New York Constitution, which provides for a three-tiered court system.

At the lowest level are the **courts of original jurisdiction**—the trial courts that are authorized to hear cases in the first instance. These courts may have either exclusive or concurrent jurisdiction over a particular matter. **Exclusive jurisdiction** means that the subject of the lawsuit may be tried only in a particular court; **concurrent jurisdiction** means that there are two or more courts that are able to adjudicate the matter.

<u>Example</u>: *Family Court in New York has the jurisdiction to determine the custody of children; however, the Surrogate's Court, the court that hears matters concerning decedents' estates, also may hear custody matters, usually if the question of the child's custody has arisen because of the death of the child's guardian. This is an example of concurrent jurisdiction.*

<u>Example</u>: *A couple who were married in and who live in New York now want to divorce. Pursuant to statute, the only court that has the power to hear and adjudicate divorce actions is the Supreme Court—its jurisdiction is exclusive in this matter.*

Four specific statutes govern the New York court system:

1. The New York City Civil and Criminal Court Act (NYCCCCA) governs civil and criminal courts in the city of New York.
2. The Unified City Court Act (UCCA) governs courts in cities other than the city of New York.
3. The Unified District Court Act (UDCA) provides for district courts according to county. To date, only Nassau and Suffolk counties have provided for district courts.
4. The Unified Judicial Court Act (UJCA) governs the overall superstructure of the court system.

Together, these four statutes create what is known as the **unified court system**.

As stated above, New York provides for a three-tiered court structure. The lowest court in the state, the court of original jurisdiction, is called the **Supreme Court**. In order to streamline the litigation process, the Supreme Court has authorized various subsidiary courts that may hear certain limited matters (*see below*).

The state is divided into four judicial departments. Appeals from the court of original jurisdiction are taken to the appellate courts by judicial department. The appellate court of first appeal is called the **Appellate Division of the Supreme Court**. For New York City and the counties of Nassau and Suffolk, appeals are taken to a court called Appellate Term. Decisions of the Appellate Term are appealed either to the Appellate Division or to the Court of Appeals, depending upon the nature of the lawsuit.

The court of last resort under the New York state court system, the highest court in the state, is the **New York Court of Appeals**. Note that, unlike most of the other jurisdictions, New York's Supreme Court is the lowest court and the highest court is the Court of Appeals.

Jurisdiction

A court may hear a case only if it has the authority to adjudicate the matter. This authority is known as the court's **jurisdiction**, the ability to hear a particular lawsuit. The concept of jurisdiction concerns two separate but intertwined issues: subject matter jurisdiction and jurisdiction over the parties to the lawsuit.

Subject Matter Jurisdiction

Subject matter jurisdiction refers to the court's ability to grant the type of relief sought. The subject matter jurisdiction of each court is set by statute, and neither the parties nor the court can waive jurisdiction. If the court is not authorized to hear a particular type of case, the suit must be dismissed. CPLR § 3211(a)(2), (e). Questions concerning the court's subject matter jurisdiction can be raised at any time during the litigation, either by the parties to the suit or by the court itself.

The subject matter jurisdiction of the New York courts is as follows:

- *Supreme Court*. The Supreme Court of New York is a court of general jurisdiction, meaning that it is authorized to hear all matters except those that arise under federal law (which must be adjudicated in a federal court). As mentioned above, in order to ease the burden of the Supreme Court, eleven subsidiary courts have been established with limited subject matter jurisdiction. However, the Supreme Court has exclusive jurisdiction in all suits concerning matrimonial issues (divorce, separation, declaration of nullity, annulment), Article 78 proceedings (claims against government officers, discussed in Chapter Eight), and declaratory judgments. However, claims against the state of New York are not heard by the Supreme Court but must be brought in the **Court of Claims**.

If a matter is filed in the Supreme Court, but should have been instituted in one of the subsidiary courts, the Supreme Court can transfer the case to the lower court and may impose a cost penalty on the party who instituted the action.

The jurisdiction of the subsidiary courts of original jurisdiction is as follows:

- <u>*County courts*</u>. A county court has been established in each of the 62 counties of the state. The county court is authorized to hear matters in which the amount in controversy does not exceed $25,000, although a few of the county courts have limited this jurisdictional amount to an amount below $25,000. Jud. L. Sec. 190(5). There is no monetary limit imposed on the jurisdiction of the county court for
  a) real estate actions for realty located in the county
  b) replevin actions
  c) summary proceedings
  d) any counterclaims brought against the plaintiff by the defendant once the plaintiff's jurisdiction has been established.

- <u>*District courts*</u>. Only Nassau and Suffolk counties have established district courts. These courts may hear matters in which the amount in controversy does not exceed $15,000. These courts have no dollar limit, however, on summary judgments, counterclaims, or real estate proceedings. The district courts have created a Small Claims Part to hear matters for amounts not exceeding $1,000.

- <u>*City courts*</u>. Except for New York City, the city court may hear matters in which the amount in controversy does not exceed $15,000. There is no limit on the amount in controversy for counterclaims or interpleaders.

- <u>*Town and village courts*</u>. These courts, sometimes referred to as the **Justice of the Peace** or the **Village Police Court**, may hear matters involving amounts up to $3,000, and may have a

Small Claims Part for cases involving no more than $500 in controversy.

- _Surrogate's courts_. There is a Surrogate's Court for each county in the state, and it has jurisdiction over the estate of decedents domiciled or resident in New York and certain trusts created during the grantor's lifetime. It also has concurrent jurisdiction with Family Court over certain custody proceedings.

- _Family courts_. There are Family Courts in every county of the state except for New York City; there is only one Family Court for the five counties composing the city of New York. Family Court has jurisdiction to hear all matters involving domestic issues except for divorce, annulment, separation, and declaration of the nullity of a marriage. Its jurisdiction is concurrent with that of the Supreme Court.

- _New York City courts_. The city of New York has its own Civil and Criminal Court. The Civil Court of the city of New York can hear claims with an amount in controversy not exceeding $25,000. The Civil Court also has a Small Claims Part to adjudicate matters involving amounts up to $3,000 and a Housing Part to determine landlord-tenant disputes.

Cases adjudicated in the New York City Civil or Criminal Court and the Long Island District Courts can be appealed to the Appellate Term. Matters initially decided by the Supreme Court, County Court, Family Court, Surrogate's Court, Court of Claims, and the Appellate Term can be appealed to the Appellate Division of the Supreme Court. Moreover, the Appellate Division has original jurisdiction to hear all matters concerning the admission and supervision of attorneys licensed to practice in the state and for Article 78 proceedings (*see* Chapter Eight).

Decisions of the Appellate Division can be appealed to the New York Court of Appeals. However, if the issue in controversy concerns the constitutionality of a state or federal statute, the problem can be appealed directly to the Court of Appeals without first seeking an intermediate appeal at the Appellate Term or Appellate Division.

Generally, appellate courts are only permitted to review lower courts' application of law to the proven facts; they have no ability to review the findings of facts as determined by the trial court. Despite this general rule, the New York Court of Appeals is authorized to review facts in two situations:

1. when the death penalty has been imposed
2. when the Appellate Division has reversed or modified a trial court decision based on a finding of new facts.

The threshold question involved in any civil lawsuit is the determination of which court has the appropriate jurisdiction to hear the case. A case may be transferred from one court to another because of a lack of subject matter jurisdiction by motion. The case may be transferred for the following reasons:

1. The original court lacked subject matter jurisdiction from the outset. A motion to the Supreme Court pursuant to CPLR § 325(a) effects the transfer.

Example: *A spouse files for divorce in Family Court. Family Court lacks the jurisdiction to hear divorce actions, and so the case must be transferred to the Supreme Court.*

2. During the proceedings matters arise that indicate that the court no longer has sufficient subject matter jurisdiction; in this case, removal is appropriate. CPLR § 325(b).

Example: *A man institutes a personal injury action in the Nassau District court seeking $15,000 in damages. During the discovery process, it is determined that the man's injuries are far more serious than first thought, and the damages will exceed $15,000 if the man is successful. This case may be removed to the Supreme Court.*

3. A court of lesser jurisdiction has the authority to hear the case. As mentioned above, if the suit was originally brought alleging an excessive amount in bad faith, simply to acquire the subject matter jurisdiction of the Supreme Court, when in fact the matter involves a lesser amount, the proceeding may be dismissed. However, if the action was commenced in good faith, but it was subsequently determined that the amount in controversy was less than originally supposed, the matter may be transferred with the consent of the parties to a lower court. CPLR § 325(a), (d).

Example: *A man from the Bronx institutes a suit in the Supreme Court based on a breach of contract, claiming damages of $50,000. Later it is discovered that the actual loss would be not more than $23,000. The suit was instituted in good faith. The matter may be removed to the New York City Civil Court.*

Remember that questions concerning the court's subject matter jurisdiction may be raised at any time, even after the verdict has been rendered, and if the court in fact did not have appropriate subject matter jurisdiction its decision will be invalid.

Even if the particular court has the authority to hear the matter, it still may not be the appropriate forum to adjudicate the dispute. This can arise if the court determines that another court, in the interests of justice, should hear the case. This concept is known as ***forum non conveniens*** (Latin for "inconvenient forum") and may be brought to the court's attention by a motion of one of the parties (CPLR § 327). Granting or denying the motion is discretionary with the court, which must weigh various factors to determine the fairness of the motion. The factors that the court uses to resolve the matter are: the inconvenience to the plaintiff, the convenience to the defendant, and the convenience of the court. Such motions are usually made if the incident in question occurred in a different county, all of the witnesses are in a different county, or because of the notoriety of the particular case it would be impossible to have an impartial hearing in the court where the action was instituted. If it is determined that it is indeed an inconvenient forum for the adjudication of the dispute the court may dismiss the action (unlikely) or stay the proceeding until the action is commenced in a different court.

Note the distinction between transferring a case because of lack of subject matter jurisdiction and a motion for *forum non conveniens*. In the former instance, the court where the suit is brought cannot hear the matter because of a lack of authority; in the latter, the court may hear the dispute, but, in the interests of fairness, believes a different court should hear the matter.

Example: *A lawsuit is instituted in Onandaga County based on an accident that occurred in Westchester County. The amount of the alleged injury is $25,000, and both parties reside in Onandaga County. Because the accident occurred in Westchester, and all of the witnesses are located in Westchester, the court may entertain a motion for* forum non conveniens *so that the case can be removed to Westchester County.*

Jurisdiction Over the Parties

Even if the court has the appropriate subject matter jurisdiction to hear the case, maintaining a lawsuit in that court would be meaningless if the court had no authority to enforce its judgment against the defendant. Therefore, in addition to subject matter jurisdiction, the court must have **personal jurisdiction** over the defendant to adjudicate a civil dispute.

Jurisdiction to enforce a judgment may be based on either **in personam jurisdiction**, **in rem jurisdiction**, or **quasi-in-rem jurisdiction**.

In Personam Jurisdiction

This refers to the court's ability to enforce a judgment against the person of the defendant. Such jurisdiction may arise in one of the following ways:

1. <u>*Physical Presence*</u>. CPLR § 308(1). The defendant is physically in the state of New York. However, mere physical presence in New York alone may not be sufficient if
   a. the plaintiff or plaintiff's agent used **fraudulent enticement** to entice the defendant into the state just to acquire jurisdiction over the defendant;
   b. the defendant entered the state voluntarily to appear before a judicial or quasi-judicial tribunal as a witness. If the defendant is appearing at a judicial hearing in New York because the defendant was subpoenaed, the defendant is not immune from the jurisdiction of the New York court;
   c. the court grants a criminal defendant limited immunity.

2. <u>*Doing Business in the State*</u>. CPLR §301. If the defendant is a domestic New York corporation, the court has jurisdiction because of the defendant's domicile (*see below*). However, if the defendant is a foreign corporation or other foreign business entity, the New York courts will have jurisdiction if
   a. the matter in controversy involves a contract to be performed in New York or concerns property located in New York;
   b. the subject matter of the lawsuit is located in New York;
   c. the claim arose in New York, except for a claim of title to property located outside of the state;
   d. the foreign business entity is
      (1) authorized to do business in New York, or
      (2) in fact doing business in New York even though not authorized to do so, or
      (3) subject to the long-arm statute (*see below*).

Furthermore, if the foreign business entity maintains a subsidiary in New York, the New York court can "pierce the corporate veil" and thus acquire jurisdiction over the parent company. If the foreign business entity has business affiliates in New York, the New York court *might* have jurisdiction depending upon whether the affiliate is an independent entity or an interested entity. If the foreign business entity has independent contractors in New York, the New York court *might* have jurisdiction over the foreign business entity depending upon the nature of the activity of the independent contractor. If the independent contractor merely solicits business for the foreign entity, the court lacks jurisdiction; however, if the independent contractor is authorized to enter into contracts on behalf of the foreign entity, the New York court may have jurisdiction.

Example: *An Iowa corporation is the sole shareholder of a New York corporation organized under the laws of the state of New York. In this instance, the Iowa corporation may be considered to be doing business in New York through its wholly owned subsidiary.*

Example: *A California corporation is a shareholder of a New York corporation, which in turn is a shareholder of the California corporation. Shareholding permits each corporation to elect directors to each other's boards (an interlocking directorate). In this instance, New York may have jurisdiction over the California corporation.*

Example: *A Florida real estate company hires a New York broker to solicit purchasers for Florida homes. The broker has no authority to sign contracts for the sale of the land on the Florida company's behalf. In this case, New York will lack personal jurisdiction over the Florida business.*

3. *Domicile*. CPLR §§ 313, 301. If a person is legally domiciled in New York, regardless of where the person actually resides, the New York court has in personam jurisdiction.

4. *Single Act or Long-Arm Statute*. CPLR § 302. The long-arm statute is a legislative enactment that permits the New York courts to acquire personal jurisdiction over a non-resident under one of the following circumstances:
   a. The cause of action arose out of an activity that took place in New York.
   b. The court has jurisdiction over the defendant or the defendant's executor, administrator, or agent if

(1) the defendant transacted business in New York or contracted to supply goods or services in New York. CPLR § 302(a)(1). Note that "transacting business" is a lesser standard than "doing business." "Transacting business" can occur just once, whereas "doing business" involves a continuing presence.

(2) the defendant committed a tortious act in New York (except for defamation and the tort incident to breach of contract). CPLR § 302(a)(3).

(3) the defendant committed a tortious act outside of New York that had effect in New York (except for defamation and the tort incident to breach of contract) [(CPLR § 302(a)(3)] if:

(a) the defendant solicits business in New York

(b) the defendant committed a tortious act outside New York that could reasonably have been expected to cause injury in New York.

(c) the defendant either owns or uses property located in New York. CPLR § 302(a)(4).

5. *Express Consent*. CPLR § 318. By agreement, the defendant contracted to be subject to the jurisdiction of the courts of New York. Under this provision New York requires the plaintiff to serve a summons on the New York Secretary of State or the defendant's resident agent in the state, or to serve the defendant by mail or in person (*see below*) to make sure that the defendant knows that he or she is being sued. (For a discussion of methods of notice, *see* Chapter Two.)

6. *Use of the New York Courts*. CPLR § 303. When a defendant seeks legal relief in the New York judicial system, either by initiating a different lawsuit or by asserting a counterclaim against the plaintiff, the defendant is deemed to have submitted to the jurisdiction of the New York courts.

7. *Implied Consent*. This method of acquiring jurisdiction applies to nonresident motorists who cause injury in New York. Under

Under this statute, the defendant has implicitly granted the New York courts jurisdiction by using the New York roadways. Vehicle and Traffic Law § 253.

8. <u>*Appearance*</u>. CPLR § 320. When a defendant voluntarily appears in a New York court to answer a complaint, unless he or she raises the question of personal jurisdiction, any objection to the court's jurisdiction is deemed waived.

In Rem Jurisdiction

A New York court can acquire in rem jurisdiction whenever property that is the subject of the lawsuit is located in the state. CPLR § 314. Because the property is in the state, the New York court has the authority to enforce judgments against the property.

<u>*Example*</u>: *A resident of North Carolina is claiming title to a house located in Rochester, New York, that she purchased from a Georgia resident. Even though both parties are outside the state, because the matter involves title to realty located in the state, the New York court has jurisdiction to hear the matter.*

Quasi-in-Rem Jurisdiction

A New York court can acquire jurisdiction over the parties if some property owned by the defendant (not the property that is the subject matter of the lawsuit) is located in New York under the concept of quasi-in-rem jurisdiction, because the New York court can enforce its judgment over the property located within its borders. This form of jurisdiction over the parties is rarely asserted.

<u>*Example*</u>: *A Texan is claiming injury caused by a breach of contract with a New Mexican resident whom the Texan can no longer locate. The only property that the Texan can locate that is owned by the New Mexican is a bank account maintained in Buffalo, New York. The New York court may entertain quasi-in-rem jurisdiction because, if*

successful, the Texan can have his claim satisfied by the funds in the New York bank.

In addition to the foregoing, New York has promulgated certain rules with respect to acquiring jurisdiction over the parties in a matrimonial action. These rules apply whenever the suit involves

- separation
- annulment
- dissolution of a marriage
- divorce
- declaration of the nullity of a marriage
- declaration of the validity or nullity of a foreign divorce.

The Supreme Court of New York will retain jurisdiction of the matter if the plaintiff either resides or is domiciled in New York *and*

- New York was the matrimonial domicile or
- a claim for support arose out of an agreement entered into New York or
- the defendant abandoned the plaintiff in New York or
- the claim for support arose under New York law.

In this instance, the plaintiff is required to notify the defendant of the pendency of the action by either

- personal delivery of such notice to the defendant
- substituted service (*see* Chapter Three)
- publication (with the leave of the court).

Statute of Limitations

Simply because a court is found to have competent jurisdiction over the subject matter and the parties to the lawsuit does not mean that the court will be able to entertain the action. In addition to the foregoing jurisdictional requirements, in order for a tribunal to hear a particular matter, it must be shown that the suit was brought within an appropriate period of time from the occurrence of the act or transaction that gave rise to the conflict. The period in which the plaintiff must institute the lawsuit is determined by the Statute of Limitations.

The rationale behind having a statutorily determined period in which to initiate a legal action is simple: a person should not have to spend a lifetime of uncertainty wondering whether he or she will have to defend a lawsuit. The period indicated by the statute is generally strictly enforced, but may be waived by consent of the parties. If the defendant does not, however, raise the statute of limitations defense, either in a pretrial motion or in the answer to the complaint, it is deemed to have been waived by the defendant.

*Example: The plaintiff initiates a breach of contact lawsuit six months after the expiration of the Statute of Limitations. The defendant moves to have the lawsuit dismissed for violating the statute. Unless the plaintiff can convince the court that there was a justifiable reason that caused the delay (*see below*), the defendant's motion will be granted and the case dismissed.*

Example: The plaintiff initiates a breach of contract lawsuit six months after the expiration of the Statute of Limitations. The defendant files an answer to the plaintiff's complaint, but does not raise the question of the Statute of Limitations. During the discovery period, the defendant feels that she will lose the lawsuit and so files a motion to dismiss the case based on the Statute of Limitations. The motion will be denied—the defendant waited too long to raise this objection.

The primary question concerning the Statute of Limitations is the determination of the statutory starting point—at what moment in time did the cause of action arise? The New York statute specifies several measuring policies used to determine when the Statute of Limitations begins or stops running.

1. Accrual is the day on which the plaintiff first has the legal right to bring the action. The Statute of Limitations starts to run on the following day.

<u>Example</u>: *The plaintiff is hit by defendants' car on May 1. At that time, the plaintiff is entitled to bring a lawsuit, so the Statute of Limitations will start to run on May 2.*

2. The Statute stops running on the day process is filed with the clerk of the court in the county in which the action is to be brought. CPLR § 203(c)(1).

<u>Example</u>: *The plaintiff in the preceding example files a complaint with a court of proper jurisdiction on September 5 of the year of the accident. The Statute of Limitations stops running on September 5.*

If, for some valid reason, the plaintiff is unable to make a timely filing with the court, the plaintiff may seek an *ex parte* order from the court to extend the filing period. An ***ex parte* motion** is an application made to the court by only one side that does not require the presence of or notice to the opposing side. The right to avail oneself of these motions is determined by statute. If the judge grants the order, the plaintiff must file with the court within five days.

<u>Example</u>: *The Statute of Limitations for a particular claim expires on August 28. The plaintiff was in the hospital on that date and was released on September 3. On September 4, the plaintiff files an* ex parte *motion with the court for leave to file suit basing the claim on her hospital stay. The judge grants the motion, so the plaintiff must file suit by September 9.*

3. The Statute stops running if the defendant is served within the statutory period, or if a codefendant is served, provided that the defendant and the codefendant are united in interest with respect to the action.

Example: A plaintiff sues a retailer and a manufacturer for injuries resulting from a malfunctioning refrigerator. Even though the retailer and manufacturer are codefendants, they are not united in interest because each will allege that the other is responsible to the plaintiff.

Example: A supplier sues a business partnership for breach of contract. The partnership has three partners, but only one is served within the statutory period. Because the partners are united in interest, (i.e., they are jointly liable on the claim), the Statute of Limitations stops running after the first partner is served.

If a codefendant should have been named (as the three partners in the preceding example) but was not, and was only added to the lawsuit after the statutory period, service is still permitted if

a. the claim against the originally-named defendant and the added defendant arose out of the same transaction
b. the defendant and codefendant are united in interest
c. the codefendant knew or should have known that the lawsuit had been initiated.

4. If a provisional remedy has been sought within the statutory period and the defendant is served within 30 days of the order granting the provisional remedy, the Statute of Limitations is not violated. (For a discussion of provisional remedies, *see* Chapter Four.)

Example: A man seeks a provisional order of lis pendens *to prevent his brother from selling the land that he claims he owns but which the brother possesses. Once the order is granted, the statutory period stops running.*

5. Order of Attachment. An **order of attachment** is a provisional remedy used to stop the person in possession of property that will be the subject of a lawsuit from destroying or removing the property from the jurisdiction until the matter can be litigated. If the court grants the order of attachment, the Statute of Limitations stops running if the defendant is served within 60

days of the order (the court may grant an extension of up to 120 days). CPLR § 213. (*See* Chapter Four.)

Example: *A man is concerned that the person to whom he has loaned some valuable property is about to sell the property without his authorization to a third party. The man seeks an order of attachment to prevent the party in possession from selling the property until the matter of ownership can be litigated. If the defendant is served within 60 days of the court's granting the order of attachment, the Statute of Limitations will stop running.*

6. *Amended Pleadings*. If the plaintiff amends the pleadings to include a claim that did not appear in the original complaint, the statute stops running on the date of service of the amended pleading; however, if the amendment was noted in the original pleading, the date of the original pleading is used to determine the period of the Statute of Limitations.

Specific Statutory Time Periods

The preceding section described when the Statute of Limitations starts and stops running. The specific periods of the Statute of Limitations for New York are as follows:

20 Years

- Actions to recover on bonds
- Actions to enforce judgments
- Actions by the state to recover real property.

10 Years

- Actions to recover real property
- Actions to annul letters patent
- Actions to redeem from a mortgage.

<u>7 Years</u>

- Actions by victims to recover from the criminals who have harmed them. The date starts from the day the crime was committed, if it was a felony and the defendant derives a profit from the crime. The victim may institute the action within three years from the discovery of the criminal's profit if the profit was made after the statutory period.

<u>6 Years</u>

- Actions for which there is no specific statutory time period, known as the **equity statute**
- Actions on an express or implied contract, except for contracts covered by Article II of the Uniform Commercial Code (three years to institute a tort action against a party who induced the breach)
- Actions on a sealed instrument
- Actions on bonds or notes secured by real property mortgages
- Actions by the state for spoliation or misappropriation of public domain
- Actions based on mistakes
- Shareholder derivative actions, or an action by a corporation against a former principal
- Actions based on fraud (or two years from the date of discovery).

<u>4 Years</u>

- Breach of contract covered by the Uniform Commercial Code

<u>3 Years</u>

- Actions against a sheriff or other officer for nonpayment of money collected on execution
- Actions on a statutorily created liability
- Replevin
- Actions for damages to real property

- Actions for personal injury or malpractice, except for medical malpractice
- Actions to annul a marriage on the grounds of fraud
- Actions based on strict tort liability.

2 Years 6 Months

- Medical malpractice actions

2 Years

- Actions for wrongful death. (Note that there is no common law right to sue for wrongful death in New York.)

1 Year 90 Days

- Tort claims against a city, county, town, village, fire, or school district. For actions against municipalities, including subdivisions thereof such as a city hospital or school, a Notice of Claim must be filed within 90 days.

1 Year

- Actions based on intentional torts
- Actions against a sheriff, coroner, or constable for official omissions
- Actions to enforce penalty of forfeiture for persons who will not prosecute
- Actions based on an arbitration award
- Actions against an officer for escape of a civil prisoner
- Actions to recover overcharge of interest or enforce a penalty for overcharge
- Actions in relation to retaliatory eviction.

4 Months

- Special proceedings under Article 78 (*see* Chapter Eight)

In addition to the foregoing, the Statute of Limitations imposes additional requirements for special types of actions:

Medical Malpractice

In order to institute an action based on medical malpractice, the plaintiff must base the action on an error relating to medical treatment or diagnosis. If the action is based on ordinary negligence of the doctor or the hospital, the statutory period is three years. There are four exceptions to this basic rule:

1. If the treatment complained of was continuous, the statute begins to run after the date of the last treatment.
2. If the action is based on a foreign object being left in the patient's body, the action must commence two and one-half years after the date of the operation, or one year after the discovery.
3. If the doctor fraudulently concealed the malpractice, the doctor can be estopped from asserting the Statute of Limitations.
4. If the action complained of involves injuries *in utero*, the fetus must have been born alive.

Architect's Malpractice

The statutory period accrues on the day when the complained of work was completed, or the day on which the relationship with the architect terminated. If a third party is injured by the architect's malpractice, the statute starts to run from the date of the injury. If the malpractice occurred ten years before the date of the injury, CPLR § 214 imposes the following procedures:

1. A notice of claim must be filed at least 90 days before commencing the action.
2. The claimant may begin discovery after the notice of claim is filed.
3. The defendant may move for a summary judgment that will be granted unless
   a. notice was served
   b. there is a substantial legal basis to believe that the defendant was negligent

c. the defendant's act proximately caused the injury.

Other Professional Malpractice

The Statute of Limitations starts running either when the work was completed or when the professional relationship was terminated.

Products Liability

If the action is based on a breach of warranty, the statute starts running on the date delivery was made. If the action is against the manufacturer, the statute starts running on the date the defendant made the delivery, not the date of sale. The statutory period is four years.

If the action is based either on negligence or strict liability, the statutory period starts running from the date of the injury, regardless of when the plaintiff first has knowledge of the injury.

If the claim is based on injuries resulting from a toxic product, the statutory period starts running either from the date of discovery or the date when the plaintiff should have discovered the injury. If, when the injury was discovered, the plaintiff did not know the cause of the injury, the plaintiff may initiate suit within one year of the discovery of the cause of the injury provided

1. the discovery of the cause occurred within five years of the discovery of the injury.
2. scientific knowledge linking the cause and the injury was not known within three years of the discovery of the injury.

There is a six-year Statute of Limitations for any claim for indemnity by the manufacturer that accrues after the manufacturer pays the plaintiff. CPLR § 213.

By agreement, the parties may shorten the statutory period for initiating a claim; however, no agreement shortening claims based on the Uniform Commercial Code may be for less than one year. Any agreement not to raise the Statute of Limitations defense is void, and after accrual of the action, the parties may agree to expand the statutory period. The court has no power to extend the period on its own.

If the statutory period has expired, but the party makes a partial payment to the injured party, or acknowledges a promise to pay damages to the injured party, the statutory period begins to run anew.

Claims accruing to nonresidents are determined by both the New York statute and the Statute of Limitations in effect in the nonresident's home state.

Tolling of the Statute

The Statute of Limitations will **toll** (stop running) because of any of the following occurrences:

1. Delivery of a summons to a sheriff or filing with the county clerk results in a 60-day tolling of the statute if the delivery is made to the "wrong" official. The delivery must be fulfilled by service on the defendant. CPLR § 203(b)(1).
2. The defendant is intentionally absent from New York, thus preventing jurisdiction over him or her.
3. The plaintiff is disabled by
   a. infancy—the statute is tolled until the plaintiff's 18th birthday or ten years from accrual of a medical malpractice cause of action.
   b. insanity—three years after the disability ceases, but in no event more than ten years from accrual.
4. Death of the potential plaintiff or defendant. The personal representative of the deceased plaintiff has one year from the date of death to institute the action; the death of the potential defendant tolls the statute for 18 months from the date of death.
5. Military service.
6. Dismissal. If the original suit is dismissed, the statute is tolled for six months after the dismissal [(CPLR § 205(a)] unless
   a. there was a judgment on the merits,

b. there was a voluntary discontinuance,
c. there was a failure to prosecute, or
d. there was a lack of personal jurisdiction.

If the dismissal was for failure to effect proper service of process, the statute is tolled for 120 days from the dismissal (15 days for cases with a four-month Statute of Limitations).

Ethical Concerns

The purpose behind having jurisdictional requirements for courts and imposing statutory periods during which the injured party must institute a lawsuit is to provide for the efficient and equitable administration of justice. However, because of a certain degree of latitude permitted under the statute, many legal professionals use these statutes to "forum shop" and to delay litigation until the last possible moment thereby frustrating the purpose of the statutes. Although such actions are perfectly legal, and may be viewed as protecting the clients' interests, in the long run they operate to hinder the legal system, delay remedies, and cause anxiety for the litigants. Simply because an action is legally permissible does not automatically mean that it is ethical, and the legal professional should attempt to resolve disputes in the most efficient manner possible.

Chapter Review

The New York court structure is divided into three levels: the court of original jurisdiction is called the Supreme Court, which has created certain subsidiary courts with limited jurisdiction to lighten the burden of the court at the trial level; courts in which an intermediary appeal may be taken, either at the Appellate Term or the Appellate Division; and the court of last resort, the highest court in the state, the New York Court of Appeals. The procedure for maintaining a civil action in these courts is contained in the New York Civil Practice Law and Rules (CPLR).

In order to institute a lawsuit in the courts of New York, three requirements must be met: the court in which the suit is brought must have jurisdiction to hear the type of action brought before it (subject matter jurisdiction); the court must have the legal ability to enforce its orders against the litigants (jurisdiction over the parties); and the action must be brought to the attention of the court within the statutory period of time. If any of these three elements is lacking, the court may not hear the case.

Key Terms

Accrual – the time at which the Statute of Limitations begins to run

Answer – the defendant's response to a complaint

Appellate Division – the intermediate court of appeals in New York

Appellate Term – the intermediate court of appeal for appeals from the first and second judicial departments

Civil Procedure Law and Rules (CPLR) – New York statutes delineating civil procedure

Complaint – document filed by the plaintiff indicating the grounds for the lawsuit

Concurrent jurisdiction – subject matter jurisdiction exercised by two or more courts simultaneously

Court of Appeals – the highest court in the state of New York

Court of Original Jurisdiction – trial court

Defendant – alleged wrongdoer

***Ex parte* order** – court order issued with only one side present

Exclusive jurisdiction – the statutory ability of only one court to hear a particular matter

Federal Rules of Civil Procedure – federal statute delineating procedure in the federal courts

Forum non conveniens – motion to have action moved to a more convenient forum

In Personam (Personal) Jurisdiction – jurisdiction over the person of the defendant

In Rem Jurisdiction – jurisdiction over the property that is the subject of the lawsuit

Jurisdiction – legal authority to hear a case

Jurisdiction over the parties – the authority to enforce orders over the litigants

Motion – request to the court

Order of attachment – provisional remedy

Plaintiff – person who institutes a civil action

Pleading – document filed with the court incident to a lawsuit

Quasi-in-rem jurisdiction – jurisdiction over property that can be used to satisfy a claim, not the property that is the subject of the lawsuit

Statute of Limitations – statutory period of time in which a lawsuit must be instituted

Subject matter jurisdiction – authority of a court to hear a particular type of claim

Supreme Court – New York court of original jurisdiction

Tolling – stopping of the Statute of Limitations

Edited Judicial Decisions

Allende v. New York City Health and Hospitals Corporation
90 NY2d 333 (1997)

Did the continuous treatment doctrine toll the 90-day period in which the plaintiff was required to file a notice of claim against the defendant New York City Health and Hospitals Corporation (HHC)? Both because plaintiff's statements and actions indicate that she did not intend to return to the site of her initial treatment and because the additional treatment she received at another HHC-owned hospital did not qualify as continuous treatment, we reverse the Appellate Division order and dismiss the complaint.

I.

On April 12, 1985, at her personal physician's recommendation, plaintiff Rosaura Allende went to the emergency room of Lincoln Hospital, complaining of a fever and back and chest pains. Lincoln is owned by HHC. Plaintiff was diagnosed with pneumonia and was admitted to Lincoln for immediate treatment. Her condition worsened, necessitating a lengthy stay, and an arterial catheter was placed in her left wrist to monitor the oxygenation of her blood.

Upon the catheter's removal, plaintiff began to experience circulation problems in her left hand. At the time these problems were first noticed, attending physicians at Lincoln considered procedures to improve the circulation but eventually rejected them because of plaintiff's weakened condition. Her left hand discolored, and her left middle and index fingertips ultimately became gangrenous.

When plaintiff was discharged on July 4, 1985, a doctor at Lincoln informed her that the gangrenous parts of her fingers would eventually dry and fall off. She was advised to return to Lincoln at that time so that her hand could be examined. The gangrenous areas of plaintiff's fingers subsequently hardened and began to chip away, but plaintiff did not return to Lincoln. At several clinics in her neighborhood which were unaffiliated with HHC she was told that they could do nothing for her hand, and that she would have to seek attention at a hospital. On December 14, 1985, the gangrenous tip of her left index finger came off but plaintiff did not return to Lincoln or seek medical attention at that time.

Plaintiff later sought care for treatment of conditions unrelated to her fingers at North Central Bronx Hospital, another HHC facility. She visited North Central three times between December 27, 1985, and January 9, 1986, and complained of pain in her left hand only on her last visit. On January 25, 1986, where her left middle finger was smashed by a window that fell as she attempted to open it, when the gangrenous portion of that finger came loose, plaintiff went to the emergency room of North Central, where doctors amputated the loose portion of the finger.

Plaintiff served a notice of claim on HHC on March 28, 1986, and commenced the instant suit, claiming that a surgical procedure, which could have saved the circulation in her left hand and prevented the ultimate loss of her two fingers, should have been performed at Lincoln.

Before trial, HHC moved to dismiss the complaint or alternatively for summary judgment on the ground that plaintiff failed to comply with the 90-day limitations period for filing a notice of claim (General Municipal Law § 50-e; McKinney's Unconsol. Laws of NY § 7401[2] [New York City Health and Hospitals Corporation Act § 20(2); L 1969, ch. 1016, § 1, as amended]). The Supreme Court denied the motion, holding that issues of fact existed concerning continuous treatment, and the Appellate Division affirmed. After trial, the jury returned a $1,000,000 verdict in plaintiff's favor.

By post-trial motion, defendant again sought to dismiss the complaint for failure to file a timely notice of claim or alternatively to set aside the verdict as excessive. The trial court denied the motion to dismiss, finding that the doctrine of continuous treatment applied. The court noted "it is undisputed that plaintiff and the physicians at Lincoln who treated her expected that she would ultimately return for further treatment to her fingers," concluding "plaintiff intended to utilize HHC facilities for her finger injuries and treatment. Indeed, plaintiff's election to seek subsequent treatment at North Central Bronx rather than Lincoln does not destroy, legally speaking, a claim of continuous treatment by HHC." The court, however, granted defendant's motion to the limited extent of finding the award for future pain and suffering to be excessive, ordering a new trial on damages unless plaintiff stipulated to a reduced award of $750,000 (which plaintiff did). The Appellate Division affirmed. We granted leave to appeal, and now reverse.

II.

A notice of claim in a medical malpractice action against HHC must be filed within 90 days after the claim arises (General Municipal Law § 50-e;

McKinney's Unconsol. Laws of N.Y. § 7401 New York City Health and Hospitals Corporation Act § 20(2); L 1969, ch 1016, § 1, as amended]). Since plaintiff failed to file such a notice until more than six months after the alleged negligence at Lincoln and never sought permission to file a late notice of claim, her claim can be saved only by the continuous treatment doctrine we first articulated in *Borgia v. City of New York* (12 NY2d 151, 155) and which was later codified in CPLR § 214-a. Under plaintiff's theory, her notice of claim was timely because it was filed within 90 days of her January 25, 1986 treatment at North Central—on March 28, 1986. There is no dispute that, if otherwise applicable to the facts of this case, the continuous treatment doctrine applies to the time in which to file a notice of claim under General Municipal Law § 50-e (*Borgia v. City of New York, supra*, 12 NY2d, at 155; *see also, Davis v. City of New York*, 38 NY2d 257).

Under the continuous treatment doctrine, "the time in which to bring a malpractice action is stayed 'when the course of treatment which includes the wrongful acts or omissions has run continuously and is related to the same original condition or complaint'" (*McDermott v. Torre*, 56 NY2d 399, 405, *quoting Borgia v. City of New York, supra*, 12 NY2d, at 155). As we have recognized, it "would be absurd to require a wronged patient to interrupt corrective efforts by serving a summons on the physician or hospital" (*Borgia v. City of New York, supra*, 12 NY2d, at 156). Further, we have noted that the doctor committing the alleged malpractice is not only in a position to identify and correct any mistakes but also best placed to do so (*Ganess v. City of New York*, 85 NY2d 733, 735; *Cooper v. Kaplan*, 78 NY2d 1103). One of the elements of continuous treatment is that

> [F]urther treatment is explicitly anticipated by both physician and patient as manifested in the form of a regularly scheduled appointment for the near future, agreed upon during that last visit, in conformance with the periodic appointments which characterized the treatment in the immediate past.... [W]here the physician and patient reasonably intend the patient's uninterrupted reliance upon the physician's observation, directions, concern, and responsibility for overseeing the patient's progress, the requirement for continuous ... treatment ... [is] satisfied. (*Richardson v. Orentreich*, 64 NY2d 896, 898–899 [emphasis added]; *see also, Cox v. Kingsboro Med. Group*, 88 NY2d 904.)

The trial court and Appellate Division found, on the facts before them, that this requirement had been satisfied—that both plaintiff and the doctors at Lincoln expected that she would return for further treatment on her fingers. Affirmed factual findings are beyond the scope of our review so long as they are supported by some evidence in the record (*see, e.g., Stiles v. Batavia Atomic Horseshoes*, 81 NY2d 950–51).

While there is ample support for the finding that the doctors at Lincoln expected plaintiff to return, there is no evidence that plaintiff herself shared that intention. Plaintiff never testified that she planned to visit Lincoln following her discharge. Quite the contrary, when asked on direct examination why she did not return to Lincoln for treatment, she stated, "[b]ecause I did not have faith any more in that hospital."

Plaintiff's actions similarly indicate that she did not intend to return to Lincoln. She sought no medical attention when part of her index finger came off in December 1985. When the window smashed her middle finger the following month, she went to North Central, not Lincoln. Plaintiff also testified that she visited other clinics after her discharge from Lincoln: "the clinic where I used to live," "Burnside Clinic," and "another one that is on 176th and Jerome." The record is therefore bereft of support for the finding that plaintiff intended "uninterrupted reliance upon [Lincoln] physician's observation, directions, concern, and responsibility for overseeing the patient's progress" (*Richardson v. Orentreich*, 64 NY2d 896, 899, *supra*).

Nor does plaintiff's situation comport with the policies behind the continuous treatment doctrine. As plaintiff herself no longer had any faith in Lincoln she cannot be said to have had the "continuing trust and confidence" in her health care providers that underlies the continuous treatment doctrine (*Richardson v. Orentreich*, *supra*, at 898, *citing Coyne v. Bersani*, 61 NY2d 939, 940). Moreover, because there is no evidence that plaintiff herself contemplated any continuity of relationship, declining to apply the continuous treatment doctrine would not "require a wronged patient to interrupt corrective efforts by serving a summons on the [negligent treatment provider]" (*Borgia v. New York*, 12 NY2d 151, 156, *supra*).

III.

Plaintiff's reliance on the continuous treatment doctrine suffers additionally from the fact that the subsequent treatment she received was at a different medical facility, by different doctors. Where the continuing treatment is provided by someone other than the allegedly negligent practitioner, there must be " 'an agency or other relevant relationship' " between the health care providers (*Meath v. Mishrick*, 68 NY2d 992, 994, *quoting McDermott v. Torre*, 56 NY2d 399, 403, *supra*). Plaintiff urges that the "relevant relationship" exists here simply because Lincoln and North Central are both owned by HHC.

Plaintiff contends that since HHC owns and operates all New York City hospitals (McKinney's Unconsol. Laws of N.Y. § 7386[1][a] [New York City Health and Hospitals Corporation Act § 6(a); L 1969, ch. 1016, § 1 (§ 6), as amended]), filing a notice of claim as to one HHC hospital would interrupt the care received at any of the facilities under its auspices and trigger the continuous treatment doctrine. We conclude, however, that HHC's ownership alone does not establish the necessary nexus.

As we have recognized in an analogous situation, an individual practitioner's affiliation with a hospital is insufficient to create a "relevant relationship" between the two (*Meath v. Mishrick*, 68 NY2d 992, 994, *supra; see also, Ruane v. Niagara Falls Mem. Med. Ctr.*, 60 NY2d 908). Mere common ownership of two hospitals by HHC is even less of a nexus. Nor does application of the doctrine here advance its underlying policies. Filing a notice of claim or the negligence of doctors at one hospital would not necessarily affect the care and treatment received at another HHC facility. The "risk that the physician-patient relationship will be destroyed" (*Rizk v. Cohen*, 73 NY2d 98, 104) simply is not present when the only factor offered is common ownership by HHC.

Taken to its extreme, the rule plaintiff advocates would allow patients to move among HHC-owned hospitals indefinitely, keeping alive the Statute of Limitations for malpractice actions. That would deny the health care provider both the repose of the Statute of Limitations (*see, McCarthy v. Volkswagen of Am.*, 55 NY2d 543, 548; *Ratka v. St. Francis Hosp.*, 44 NY2d 604, 612) and the opportunity to detect and correct any prior negligent care (*Ganess v. City of New York*, 85 NY2d 733, 735, *supra*; *Cooper v. Kaplan,* 78 NY2d 1103, *supra*).

We do not foreclose the possibility that continuous treatment can exist between two hospitals owned by the same entity under the appropriate circumstances (*cf.*, *Cotto v. City of New York*, 99 AD2d 748; *Marabello v. City of New York*, 99 AD2d 133, 145 [Weinstein, J., concurring]), and save that issue for another day. However, where, as here, the only factor showing a relationship between the health care providers is their joint ownership by HHC, we decline to apply the continuous treatment doctrine. Accordingly, the order of the

Appellate Division should be reversed, with costs, and the complaint dismissed.

In the Matter of New York County DES Litigation
202 AD2d 6 (1994)

This case involves the question of whether defendant-appellant Boyle & Co. Pharmaceuticals (Boyle) is subject to the personal jurisdiction of the New York courts. It is a given that plaintiffs' mothers ingested DES in New York and that plaintiffs were *in utero* in New York when the exposure to DES took place. It is also accepted that Boyle is a closely held California corporation which manufactured and sold DES in the states west of the Mississippi from 1949 to 1960. It has never maintained an office, held a license or been registered to do business in New York, or even placed an advertisement in New York. Further, it claims that it never directly sold DES in New York or shipped it here, and for the purposes of this appeal, we accept those claims as true.

While the traditional contacts which determine jurisdiction are not present in Boyle, under the unique circumstances presented herein, the "liberal" language of the "long-arm statute," [CPLR § 302(a)(3)(ii)], can be employed to confer jurisdiction that is consistent with the Due Process Clause of the United States Constitution and even our own State's hesitancy in expanding New York's theoretical jurisdiction to its outermost limits (*see, Talbot v. Johnson Newspaper Corp.*, 71 NY2d 827, 829–830). We find that defendant Boyle realistically does have "certain minimum contacts with [New York] such that the maintenance of the suit does not offend 'traditional notions of fair play and substantial justice' " (*International Shoe Co. v. Washington*, 326 U.S. 310, 316, *quoting Milliken v. Meyer*, 311 U.S. 457, 463). We also find that the Court of Appeals would conclude that, in the area of DES product liability, and under the circumstances present here, the New York long-arm statute would provide for in personam jurisdiction (*Talbot v. Johnson Newspaper Corp.*, *supra*, at 829–830).

Section 302(a)(3)(ii) provides that "a court may exercise personal jurisdiction over any nondomiciliary ... who in person or through an agent ... (3) commits a tortious act without the state causing injury to person or property within the state ... if he ... (ii) expects or should reasonably expect the act to have consequences in the state and derives substantial revenue from interstate or international commerce."

The plaintiffs are proceeding on a "market share" theory of liability because they are unable to link the ingestion of DES (diethylstilbestrol) by their mothers during their pregnancies to any specific manufacturer (*see, Matter of DES Mkt. Share Litig.*, 79 NY2d 299; *Hymowitz v. Eli Lilly & Co.*, 73 NY2d 487, *cert. denied* 493 U.S. 944). In Hymowitz, the Court of Appeals noted that "extant common-law doctrines, unmodified, provide no relief for the DES plaintiff unable to identify the manufacturer of the drug that injured her," but concluded that these circumstances "call for recognition of a realistic avenue of relief for plaintiffs injured by DES" and that "judicial action is again required to overcome the 'inordinately difficult problems of proof' caused by contemporary products and marketing techniques [citations omitted]" (*supra*, at 507). Finding that the DES situation was "a singular case" and an "unusual scenario" (*supra*, at 508), the Court said:

> Consequently, for essentially practical reasons, we adopt a market share theory using a national market. We are aware that the adoption of a national market will likely result in a disproportion between the liability of individual manufacturers and the actual injuries each manufacturer caused in this State. Thus, our market share theory cannot be founded upon the belief that, over the run of cases, liability will approximate causation in this State [citation omitted]. Nor does the use of a national market provide a reasonable link between liability and the risk created by a defendant to a particular plaintiff [citations omitted]. Instead, we choose to apportion liability so as to correspond to the overall culpability of each defendant, measured by the amount of risk of injury each defendant created to the public-at-large. Use of a national market is a fair method, we believe, of apportioning defendants' liabilities according to their total culpability in marketing DES for use during pregnancy. Under the circumstances, this is an equitable way to provide plaintiffs with the relief they deserve, while also rationally distributing the responsibility for plaintiffs' injuries among defendants. (S*upra*, at 511–512).

As is readily apparent and, indeed, explicitly recognized (*see*, *supra*) by the Court of Appeals, Hymowitz departs from traditional common-law principles to achieve its goal of giving relief to injured DES plaintiffs. In *Matter of DES Mkt. Share Litig.* (*supra*), the Court later stressed that the new market share rule was "compelled by simple fairness' and reaffirmed that it had "relaxed" the element of proximate cause that would have required the plaintiffs to "identify the manufacturer[s] of the drug ingested by their mothers" (*supra*, at 306–307).

Since the traditional substantive rules were relaxed to allow recovery against a defendant with a national market share of the DES distribution although there was no proof that the defendant ever sold DES in New York, it would be anomalous to preclude recovery against such defendant on procedural grounds.

In any event, Boyle's involvement in this litigation is not the result of random, fortuitous or attenuated contacts with the national DES market. By its own admission, Boyle had some .3 percent of the national market. In both *Hymowitz* and *Matter of DES Mkt. Share Litig.*, the focus for substantive liability was not on a nexus with the manufacturer's New York share of the market, but the contemplated focus was with the nexus for the national market for DES.

Boyle was one of 12 manufacturers that filed New Drug Applications with the Food and Drug Administration for permission to market diethylstilbestrol for use in pregnancy. It and a small number of other pharmaceutical companies were instrumental in getting FDA approval to market DES despite the well-known fact that substances given to a pregnant woman would pass through the placenta into the fetus. In fact, as we have previously noted, as early as 1939, it was shown the administration of DES on rats and mice had malforming effects on the fetus (*see*, *Bichler v. Eli Lilly & Co.*, 79 AD2d 317, 323). Thus, Boyle, by its acts, together with other manufacturers, affirmatively interposed itself into the New York market and "should [have] reasonably expect[ed] the act to have consequences in the state" of New York (CPLR § 302[a][3][ii]).

In a long and scholarly opinion (exhaustive and authoritative enough to constitute a significant law review article) dealing with the issue before us, which was relied upon by the IAS Court, Judge Jack B. Weinstein of the Federal District Court held:

> Cases holding that jurisdiction cannot be asserted where a product's contact with New York was only through the stream of national commerce and unintended by the manufacturer are not relevant to the present case. Each involved traditional tort suits by individual plaintiffs against individual providers of goods and services [citations omitted]. *Hymowitz* is not a traditional tort case. It is the

> New York courts' response to what would otherwise be the intractable nature of the DES mass tort. Local businesses, or foreign businesses whose products normally have no contact with the United States, may arguably rely on the fact that they never expected to have any dealings that affect New Yorkers. But the same is not true of manufacturers of generic goods participating in a national industry and market ...
>
> *Hymowitz* and the New York Civil Practice Law and Rules as well as legislative policy must thus be read as favoring a jurisdictional reach consistent with the national market share rationale and the adoption of several liability. A consonant interpretation of CPLR § 302(a)(3)(ii) supports the conclusion that any manufacturer of DES, by its participation in the national marketing of a generic drug, should 'reasonably expect' its act of selling in the national market 'to have,' as CPLR § 302(a)(3)(ii) puts it, 'consequences in the state.' (*In re DES Cases [Ashley v. Abbott Labs.]*, 789 F. Supp. 552, 571–572, *appeal dismissed* 7 F.3d 20.)

Accordingly, the order of the Supreme Court, New York County (Ira Gammerman, J.), entered on or about May 4, 1993, which, insofar as appealed from, denied defendant-appellant Boyle & Co. Pharmaceuticals' motion to dismiss the complaints of plaintiffs Chernosky, Kluge and Vilasi for lack of personal jurisdiction, and order of the same court and Justice, entered on or about November 5, 1993, which deemed the above order to include the complaints of plaintiffs Carrano, Goldstein, Hooper, Shaffer and Steinberg, should be affirmed, without costs or disbursements.

Exercises

1. Why do you think there is a shorter statute of limitations for medical malpractice claims than for other torts? Explain.

2. What is your opinion of New York having subsidiary courts of original jurisdiction? Explain.

3. Why is jurisdiction over the parties limited to questioning the courts' jurisdiction over the defendant?

4. How could you document the date on which an injury was discovered for the purpose of accrual?

5. What is your opinion of New York's three-tiered court system? Explain.

Chapter Two

COMMENCEMENT OF A LAWSUIT

Introduction

To begin a civil action in the state of New York, the potential plaintiff must demonstrate two things to the court: one, the state court has jurisdiction over the potential defendant, a requirement that ensures the court's ability to enforce its ultimate decision; and two, that the potential plaintiff has notified the opposing party that a lawsuit has been filed against him or her.

As discussed in Chapter One, there are basically five factors that could give New York state courts jurisdiction over the defendant.

1. The defendant is domiciled, resident, or working in New York.
2. The defendant committed a purposeful act in New York that gave rise to the cause of action.
3. A financial benefit will accrue in New York for the defendant.
4. The defendant committed a wrongful act outside of the state, but that act has an effect on a New York resident or domiciliary.
5. The defendant engaged in a commercial transaction that affects persons who are domiciled or resident in New York.

Once it is determined that the New York court is the appropriate forum in which to bring the action, the plaintiff must file a complaint in the appropriate New York court. The complaint must detail the basis of the cause of action, and must notify the named defendant by serving on the defendant a document called a **summons** with either a copy of the complaint or a **notice** of the institution of the lawsuit. The CPLR specifies the methods by which the plaintiff is permitted to notify a defendant of a pending lawsuit, and the plaintiff must demonstrate to the court's satisfaction that the defendant has in fact been served in an appropriate manner. This demonstration of the court's ability to enforce its judgment against the defendant plus appropriate notice to the defendant pursuant to the New York statute will permit the court to entertain the lawsuit (which New York court has subject matter jurisdiction to hear the suit has been discussed in Chapter One).

The paralegal is generally responsible for drafting the initial summons and complaint or notice and for ensuring that an appropriate agency is employed to serve the defendant in the proper manner. Occasionally, the paralegal will be called upon to serve the papers on the defendant. The paralegal may then prepare an **affidavit of service** for the court as proof that the defendant has been properly served, and the paralegal is responsible for filing these documents with the clerk's office of the appropriate New York court.

Service of Process

The term **service of process** refers to the procedure for giving legal notice to a defendant that a lawsuit has been filed against him or her. A civil action commences when a summons and complaint or notice has been filed in the clerk's office of the appropriate court (*see* Chapter One) and an index number has been purchased. A **complaint** details the facts that gave rise to the lawsuit and states the relief the plaintiff is seeking. The **summons** is a document issued by the court requiring the defendant to appear before the court to answer the claims asserted against him or her in the complaint. A **notice** is a document that merely indicates the parties to the lawsuit and the fact that suit has been filed against the defendant. Chapter Three will discuss the actual preparation of these documents, whereas this chapter will focus on the requisite methods of having these documents served on the defendant.

Complaint and Notice

Pursuant to CPLR § 304, the plaintiff must file either a summons and complaint or a summons and a notice with the clerk of the court at which time the plaintiff must purchase an index number from the clerk's office. CPLR § 306-a. The fee for the index number may be waived or reduced if the plaintiff obtains a "poor person's" order from an *ex parte* justice. The **index number** indicates the date on which the summons was filed (for purposes of the Statute of Limitations, *see* Chapter One) and the number must be placed on the summons before the defendant is served. CPLR § 305(a). Thereafter, all documents relating to the specific case will be referenced by the index number. The failure to purchase an index number or place it on the summons is a filing defect.

<u>Example</u>: *A landlord wants to sue his commercial tenant for nonpayment of rent. The landlord retains an attorney who has her paralegal draft a summons and complaint for the client. The paralegal then goes to the clerk's office of the Supreme Court (the amount in controversy exceeds $30,000) and purchases an index number from the clerk which she then affixes to the summons and notes it in the case file. From this point on the matter has been filed and all reference to the case will be by the index number.*

Once the summons and complaint or notice has been filed and the index number purchased, the plaintiff is required to send notice of the lawsuit to the defendant within 120 days or, if the matter has a four-month Statute of Limitations (*see* Chapter One), within 15 days of the expiration of the statutory period. The plaintiff must file proof of service with the court.

Adequate notice to the defendant is required both for fulfilling Constitutional guarantees of due process and to comply with the specifics of the New York statute. The summons and complaint or notice may be served by any person over the age of eighteen who is a state resident and not a party to the action, CPLR § 2103(a). This person is generally referred to as the process server. Service may not be made on a Sunday (or on the defendant's Sabbath if done maliciously), but the defendant may be served on a legal holiday provided that the holiday does not fall on a Sunday.

<u>Example</u>: *The defendant in a lawsuit is an orthodox Jew who observes Saturday as his Sabbath. The plaintiff specifically insists that the process server serve the summons on Saturday. Because this is done maliciously, such service will not be deemed to have provided the defendant with proper notice.*

Methods of Service

The CPLR authorizes five different methods of service:

1. <u>Personal Service</u>. Service of process by personal delivery, the favored method of service, means that the process server leaves the document with the defendant. All other methods of service are referred to as **substituted service**.

<u>Example</u>: *The process server knocks on the defendant's door and asks for the defendant by name. The person who answers the door says that she is the person so sought, and the process server hands her the summons and notice. The defendant has been properly served by personal delivery.*

2. <u>Leave and Mail</u>. The summons and complaint or notice may be left with a person of appropriate age at the defendant's last known address or actual place of business; in addition, a copy of the documents must be mailed to the defendant within 20 days of the delivery at the place of abode or business. This form of service may only be used after personal service has been attempted at least two times on two separate occasions. The mailing must be by first-class mail, and if it is sent to the defendant's place of business, the envelope must be marked "Personal and Confidential." If there are multiple defendants, such mailing must be made to each. For lower court actions, both the leaving and mailing must occur before the Statute of Limitations expires on the cause of action.

<u>Example</u>: *The process server goes to the defendant's office to serve her with the summons and notice. The receptionist says the defendant is*

away on a business trip. The process server leaves a copy of the summons and notice with the office receptionist, and then goes to the post office and mails a copy of the documents to the defendant at the defendant's office address, marking the envelop "Personal and Confidential." The defendant has been properly served.

Proof of service must be filed with the clerk of the court within 20 days of the leaving or mailing, whichever occurs last, and service is deemed complete ten days after filing the proof of service. Leave and mail service is only permitted after personal service has been attempted on the defendant and failed. For matrimonial actions, leave and mail service is only permitted with leave of the court.

3. Service on a Designated Agent. Pursuant to CPLR § 318, if the defendant had previously authorized a person to be his or her designated agent for service of process, the plaintiff may serve the agent rather than the defendant personally.

Example: *In its Certificate of Incorporation, a New York corporation had designated its corporate Secretary as agent for service of process. The summons may be legally served by serving the corporate Secretary.*

4. Nail and Mail. If none of the preceding methods of service can be effectuated, the plaintiff may affix a copy of the summons and complaint or notice on the defendant's door and then mail a copy of the documents to the defendant by first-class mail to the defendant's last known address. This form of service is disfavored, and is only considered appropriate if the other methods have proven to be fruitless.

Example: *A landlord wants to sue his tenant for nonpayment of rent. Several attempts have been made to serve the defendant personally, but the defendant has never answered the door. The building does not have anyone with whom the papers may be left for the defendant. Under these circumstances, the landlord may be permitted to affix the papers to the tenant's door and then mail a copy to the tenant by first-class mail.*

5. Expedited Service. Expedited service may only be done with leave of the court. The plaintiff must make an *ex parte* motion to the court indicating why the other methods of service have failed and request a different method of service. CPLR § 308(5).

Example: *A plaintiff has attempted to serve the defendant on numerous occasions but every effort has failed. The Statute of Limitations to bring the suit is running out. In an* ex parte *motion, the plaintiff requests leave to serve the defendant by publication in a newspaper. In this instance, the court may grant such service.*

Special Service Procedures

There are certain rules that have been formulated to cover cases where the defendant is in a special situation.

- *Persons with Disabilities*. If the defendant is an infant (under age 18) personal service may be made on the infant's parent, guardian, or spouse. If the infant is over the age of 14, the infant defendant must be served as well. CPLR § 309(a).

Example: *A retailer intends to sue a 16-year-old for breach of contract for necessaries. The retailer must serve the defendant's parent and serve the defendant as well.*

If the defendant is a legally adjudicated incompetent, the plaintiff must serve the incompetent's appointed committee, conservator, or guardian as well as the incapacitated person. CPLR § 309(b).

No default may be entered against an infant or an incompetent until 20 days after a representative has been appointed and approved by the court. Also, a *guardian ad litem* must be appointed for an infant or an incompetent, and court approval is required to settle any claim against such persons. A *guardian ad litem* is a person appointed by the court to represent the interests of an infant or an incompetent.

- *Out-of-State Defendants*. The out-of-state defendant must be served in the same manner as an in-state defendant as indicated above, or may be served in any manner authorized by the law of the state where the defendant is domiciled or residing. CPLR § 313.

Example: A New York plaintiff wishes to sue an out-of-state defendant for a cause of action that arose in New York. The defendant's home state permits service by registered mail without any attempt of personal delivery. The New York plaintiff may serve the out-of-state defendant in this manner, and it will be deemed adequate by the New York court.

- *Corporations*. Pursuant to CPLR § 311, a corporation authorized to do business in New York may be served by personal delivery on its officers, directors, managers or general agents, cashiers or assistant cashiers, or any other person designated by the corporation as its agent for service of process. Furthermore, the corporation may be served by serving the New York Secretary of State with duplicate copies of the documents. If authorized by the court, under exceptional circumstances, corporations may be served by expedited service.

  If the corporation is not authorized to do business in the state of New York service may be effectuated by serving the New York Secretary of State and mailing a copy or serving the corporation in its home state pursuant to New York's long-arm statute (*see* Chapter One).

- *Partnerships*. Partnerships may be served by personal service on the partners, delivery or affixing the papers to the place of business and mailing a copy to the partners by first class mail, delivery on the partner or an agent of the partnership or by expedited service if authorized by the court. A partnership may be sued in the partnership name.

- *Unincorporated Associations*. An unincorporated association must be sued in the name of the President or Treasurer, and service must be made on the named individual in any manner authorized by the CPLR.

- *Public Entities*. CPLR § 311 authorizes the following methods of service on public entities:
  1. To serve a city, service must be made on the city's corporation counsel or any person authorized by the city to accept service on its behalf.
  2. To serve a court, service must be made on any judge of the court.
  3. To serve a board or council, service must be made on the presiding officer.

When any method of service is employed that requires a mailing, the mailing must be made by first-class mail, return receipt requested. The defendant must return the receipt within 30 days of receipt of the mail. If no receipt is returned, process may be made by one of the other methods.

After service, the plaintiff is required to file an affidavit of proof of service with the clerk of the court within 120 days after filing the summons and complaint or notice (15 days for claims with a four-month Statute of Limitations) and within 20 days of leaving or mailing the papers.

Example: The plaintiff files a summons and complaint with the clerk of the court on March 1. Service must be completed by June 29 (120 days after filing). The plaintiff serves on the defendant on May 2. The plaintiff must file proof of service with the clerk by May 22 (20 days after service).

Appearance

Once a defendant has been legally served, the defendant is required to make an appearance with the court to avoid default. The defendant may make an appearance by authorized representative or, if a natural person, may appear *pro se* (i.e., on his or her own behalf). Note that a corporation may only make an appearance by an attorney. The manner in which the defendant must appear depends upon the nature of the documents with which the defendant was served.

- *Summons and Notice*. To avoid default, the defendant must either request a copy of the complaint (CPLR § 3012) or serve a notice of appearance with the court. The defendant must respond within 30 days if he or she was personally served, or within 30 days of the effective date of the substituted service. The plaintiff must send a copy of the complaint to the defendant within 20 days of the request or the suit may be dismissed (CPLR § 3012). After the defendant has been served with the complaint, the defendant must either file an answer to the complaint or make a motion to the court within 20 days (*see* Chapter Four).

- *Summons and Complaint*. If the defendant was served with a summons and complaint, the defendant must either file an answer or a motion within 20 days of receipt if service was by personal service or within 30 days if another method of service was used. If mailed service was used the defendant must appear within 20 days after mailing the acknowledgment of receipt.

Making an appearance with the court does not mean that the defendant has waived any jurisdictional question, but neither does it cure a jurisdictional defect that may exist. The defendant may raise an objection to the court's jurisdiction over him or her either in a pretrial motion or in the answer to the complaint. If the objection is not made in either document, the jurisdictional challenge is deemed waived. Recall, however, that if the challenge is to the lack of the court's subject matter jurisdiction it may be raised at any time in the proceedings.

Example: The defendant has no contacts with the state of New York. In his answer to the complaint, he failed to question the court's jurisdiction over him. During the discovery process, he realizes that the court lacks jurisdiction over him. At this point, the matter is deemed waived because he failed to challenge the personal jurisdiction in his answer.

If the court denied the defendant's challenge to its jurisdiction, the defendant may appeal the ruling immediately or wait until the trial court's verdict. If the defendant does not raise the objection, it is waived.

The defendant may move to have the action dismissed if the service of process was not effectuated according to the statutory standards, but the challenge to the method of service is deemed waived if it is not made within 60 days of the service or the defendant's answer. CPLR § 3211(e). If the motion is made and found valid, the defendant will be granted a summary judgment (*see* Chapter Seven).

If the defendant files an appearance without challenging the court's jurisdiction, it is deemed a waiver to the court's in personam jurisdiction over the defendant for all matters that appear in the original complaint. However, if the plaintiff later amends the complaint, the defendant may challenge the court's jurisdiction over any additional cause of action appearing in the amended complaint.

Venue

Venue refers to the specific location of the courthouse in which the lawsuit is to be heard. There are 62 Surrogate's Courts in the state of New York. In which one should the matter be heard? Generally, the plaintiff's choice of venue prevails unless challenged by the defendant.

There are four venue categories:

1. <u>*Local*</u>. For real property actions, the venue is where the property is. (CPLR § 507).
2. <u>*Transitory*</u>. If the cause of action is transitory, it can be brought in the County in which either party resides; if neither party is a

New York resident, it can be brought in any county in the state. CPLR § 503.

3. *Replevin*. Replevin is an action to recover personal property and is deemed either local or transitory at the plaintiff's option. CPLR § 508.
4. *Contract Choice*. If the parties have contracted to specify a particular venue for any action arising out of the contract, their agreement will prevail. CPLR § 501.

The defendant may challenge the venue under the following circumstances:

1. *As of Right*. If the plaintiff has violated one of the venue categories, the defendant may make a demand for a change of venue. If the plaintiff does not consent within five days of the demand, the defendant may move for a change of venue within 15 days after the plaintiff does not consent. CPLR § 511.

Example: The plaintiff filed an action to quiet title to real property. The plaintiff filed in Albany County where the plaintiff and defendant both reside, but the property is located in Monroe County. The defendant demands a change of venue, and the plaintiff fails to consent. Within 15 days after the plaintiff's failure to consent, the defendant may move to have the matter moved to Monroe County.

2. *Discretionary*. The court has the discretion to change the venue of the lawsuit if it believes it will be impossible to have an impartial trial in the current venue or if a change of venue would be more convenient for the witnesses. CPLR § 510(2).

Example: A man has just been acquitted of murdering a young couple in a well-publicized trial. The victims' families are now suing the man in a civil action for wrongful death. Because the trial will take place in the same county in which the criminal proceeding was held, the court agrees to move the case to a different county to have an impartial trial.

Note that a special rule applies to consumer credit matters. For these lawsuits, the case may be tried either where the defendant resides or where the transaction took place, and the summons must state at the top that it is a consumer credit action.

Parties

In order to ensure complete adjudication of the cause of action, all parties to the lawsuit must be named and served. The legislature and the courts have enumerated various rules to determine who must, or who may, be named in a lawsuit and how they must be served.

Mandatory Joinders

A **mandatory joinder** means that the following categories of persons must be named as parties to the action to afford a complete adjudication of the matter

- joint obligors
- joint obligees
- the corporation in a shareholders' derivative suit
- parties claiming ownership to the property in question
- joint venturers
- beneficiaries of a trust.

All necessary parties must be joined in an action, but dismissal of the action is required only if the presence of the absentee party is indispensable to the lawsuit. Substantive, not procedural, law determines whether a party is deemed indispensable.

<u>Example</u>: *A disgruntled shareholder wants to bring a shareholder derivative suit against the directors for breach of a fiduciary duty. The complaint failed to name the corporation as a party. In order to adjudicate the matter completely the corporation must be named as a party to the suit for it to go forward.*

Permissive Joinders

Under CPLR § 1002 certain persons may be joined to a lawsuit if

- they share a common question of law or fact with the named parties
- the additional parties have a cause of action that arose out of the same transaction or series of transactions.

The "common question" need not arise out of the same cause of action, as long as the joinder of the parties would serve the efficient administration of justice. However, if necessary, the court can sever the action in circumstances it deems appropriate.

Example: *A woman has been the victim of what she believes to be medical malpractice. During discovery it is determined that the physician was never licensed, and had practiced without a license for six months prior to the institution of this lawsuit. Several other people have also suffered as a consequence of the person's treatments. These persons* may *join in the malpractice action (if they decide to) because they all share a common question of fact and law.*

Class Actions

A class action is a special type of proceeding that is authorized under Article 9 of the CPLR when the following circumstances are present:

- The parties involved are so numerous that a joinder of parties would be inappropriate.
- Common questions of law or fact predominate.
- A representative of all the parties can adequately protect the parties' interests.
- The representative's claim is typical of all other claims.
- A class action is superior to any other form of lawsuit.
- Class members have no interest in individual control of separate actions.
- Separate actions would be impracticable.

- No other relevant litigation on the matter is pending.
- It is desirable to consolidate all of the class.
- A class action would be manageable.

If the foregoing criteria are met, the action is deemed appropriate for class action status. Within 60 days of bringing the class action suit, the representative party must move the court for a judicial determination that the case may proceed as a class action. If the court agrees, the action may go forward and may not be dismissed or compromised without the approval of the court.

Example: *An airline crash kills 176 passengers. Rather than maintaining 176 separate actions for wrongful death against the airline, the lawsuit can be brought by a representative plaintiff as a class action.*

"Reasonable notice," as the court directs, must be made to all members of the class if

- the action is for injunctive or declaratory relief
- it is needed to protect the members of the class and the cost is not prohibitive.

Members of the class may "opt out" of the action if the court has no personal jurisdiction over them for lawsuits seeking monetary relief, but they may not opt out of actions seeking equitable remedies.

Third Party Practice

In **third party practice,** a defendant brings an individual into a lawsuit in the belief that that he or she is responsible, in whole or in part, for the plaintiff's claim. The defendant must prepare and file a third party summons and complaint with the clerk of the court and pay a filing fee. The third party must be served with the summons, complaint, and all other papers filed with the court regarding the action within 120 days after the initial filing of the third party claim in the same manner as is required for the original service. The third party or the original plaintiff may move to have the third party action dismissed.

In third party actions, the defendant stands in the place of a plaintiff with respect to the third party. The rationale of third party practice is that the third party is answerable if and only if the defendant is liable to the plaintiff. The basis of the third party action is that the third party may have to indemnify the defendant for any money that the defendant would have to pay the plaintiff because of an agreement or consensual relationship that exists between the defendant and the third party. The third party must answer within 20 days of service of the summons and complaint, and can assert any defense the defendant has against the plaintiff as well as any counterclaim he or she may have against the defendant (*see* Chapter Three).

The third party's answer must be served on both the defendant and the plaintiff, and the plaintiff may amend the original complaint within 20 days of service on him or her of the third party's answer without leave of court.

If the basis of the case is for workers' compensation, the plaintiff may sue the third party but the third party is precluded from suing the employer unless the plaintiff was *gravely* injured. For joint tortfeasors, each is liable fully for any economic loss suffered by the injured party, but is only liable for his or her portion of any noneconomic loss. The noneconomic loss provision does not apply to

- injuries resulting from reckless disregard of safety
- strict liability cases
- motor vehicle accidents
- releasing hazardous substances into the atmosphere.

Example: A customer falls in a store owned by a partnership. As a result of the accident the customer has lost wages and incurred medical expenses of $30,000, and is suing for $250,000 total to compensate for pain, suffering and mental anguish. She only named one of the three partners in the lawsuit because the partners are jointly and severally *liable for tort claims. The named defendant serves his two partners as third parties. If the plaintiff is successful, each partner is liable for $10,000 representing the plaintiff's economic loses, but the court must determine the degree of responsibility attributable to each partner for the plaintiff's noneconomic loss.*

When a defendant brings in a third party, or a plaintiff brings in a third party because of a counterclaim asserted by the defendant (*see* Chapter Three), it is called **impleading**.

Interpleader

An **interpleader** is a form of action in which the plaintiff was injured, but does not know which of several defendants caused the injury or to what extent each might be liable. The plaintiff will interplead the multiple defendants and let the defendants argue among themselves to determine liability.

Example: *A man is injured when a toaster he bought explodes. He interpleads the retailer and the manufacturer, not knowing which is liable for the malfunction. In court, the retailer and the manufacturer will attempt to prove the other is responsible for the plaintiff's injuries.*

Intervention

Intervention is a process in which a person not a party to the action wishes to participate because he believes that the outcome of the lawsuit will have some effect on him. Intervention may be by right, if the intervenor will be directly affected by the action, or by permission of the court if the intervenor will be only incidentally affected.

Example: *A lawsuit has been filed with respect to title to property. A person who had leased the property wishes to intervene because the outcome of the lawsuit will affect her rental obligations.*

Ethical Concerns

Historically, many ethical problems have been associated with service of process issues. The CPLR has promulgated specific rules and regulations with respect to service of process so that situations in which parties to a lawsuit employ ineffective methods of notification in order to have default judgments entered against defendants could be avoided. At one time New York was noted for its "sewer service," in which plaintiffs threw summonses into the sewer claiming that they had sent it along to the defendant. Current practices and procedures preclude such occurrences.

Because the CPLR imposes time restrictions, many attorneys wait until the last possible moment in which to file documents, using the time delay to annoy the opposing side. Although such time delays are not legal violations, they may be viewed as an unnecessary, if not unethical, legal practice.

Chapter Review

In order to initiate a lawsuit in the courts of New York, a potential plaintiff must file a summons and complaint or notice with the clerk of the appropriate court and purchase an index number from the clerk. The index number must appear on the face of the summons and all subsequent papers filed with the court concerning the action. Once filed with the court it is the plaintiff's obligation to see that the defendant is adequately notified of the proceedings. Such notification is effectuated by the service of process on the defendant.

New York authorizes five methods of service of process. The most favored method is personal service on the defendant. If personal service cannot be made, the plaintiff may use one of the following methods of substituted service: leave and mail, nail and mail, service on an authorized agent, or expedited service with leave of the court. Once served, the plaintiff must file proof of service with the court within a statutorily defined period.

Once served, the defendant is required to appear before the court. The defendant may do so either by motion to dismiss the case or by answering the plaintiff's complaint. Failure to appear may result in a default judgment being entered against the defendant.

In order to ensure complete adjudication, all necessary parties to the action must be joined. In certain circumstances, if the number of plaintiffs would be excessively high, the court may allow a representative plaintiff to bring suit as a class action. A defendant is also permitted to bring into the lawsuit third parties that the defendant believes are legally liable for all or part of the plaintiff's alleged injuries.

Key Terms

Affidavit of service – notarized document stating that the defendant has been served with a summons and complaint or notice

Class action – lawsuit brought by a representative plaintiff when the number of potential plaintiffs is extremely high

Complaint – pleading that alleges the facts, cause of action, and relief alleged by the plaintiff

Expedited service – substituted service permitted by the court in limited circumstances

Guardian ad litem – fiduciary appointed by the court to represent interests of incompetent persons during litigation

Implead – bringing in a third party

Index number – number that must be purchased from the clerk of the court to identify lawsuits

Interpleader – situation in which the plaintiff sues multiple defendants not knowing who may be liable and the defendants argue the matter of liability among themselves

Intervention – voluntarily entering into a lawsuit because the intervenor may be affected by the outcome

Mandatory joinder – the practice of including persons in a lawsuit to ensure complete adjudication

Notice – notification of a pending lawsuit

Permissive joinder – a person who may be included in a lawsuit because he or she has issues in common with the litigants

Process server – person who delivers pleadings to parties in a lawsuit

Replevin – action to recover personal property

Service of process – method of bringing the defendant a summons and complaint or notice of lawsuit

Summons – court document requiring that the defendant appear in court

Venue – physical location of the appropriate court

Edited Judicial Decisions

Vincenzino v. Calvosa v. NYSA-ILA Medical Center
151 Misc. 2d 95 (1991)

The third-party defendant moves for an order, under CPLR § 3211(a)(7), dismissing the third-party complaint for failure to state a cause of action.

Plaintiff Mario Vincenzino commenced this action claiming that on May 3, 1989, defendant George Calvosa provoked an argument with him at NYSA-ILA Medical Center, pointed a loaded gun at him and threatened to shoot him.

Vincenzino alleges that Calvosa's actions caused him to sustain severe personal injuries and emotional distress. In his third-party complaint Calvosa impleads NYSA-ILA Medical Center and alleges that Vincenzino was an employee of the medical center but that he was unstable and unsuited for his employment. Calvosa's third-party complaint also alleges that Vincenzino had a propensity for violence and that the third-party defendant knew of such propensity. Calvosa claims "that if the plaintiff sustained the injuries as alleged in the Complaint, then the said incident came about solely and wholly by reason of the recklessness, carelessness and negligence of the third-party defendant" in negligently hiring the plaintiff (third-party complaint, para. 15).

The courts of this state have long recognized a cause of action for negligent hiring (*see Vandehule v. Berinstein*, 285 App. Div. 290, *amended on other grounds*, 284 App. Div. 1039).

To recover damages for injuries sustained because an employer has hired or retained an incompetent employee, a plaintiff must establish a duty owed by the defendant employer to the plaintiff, a breach of that duty and damages proximately caused by the defendant employer's breach (29 Am. Jur. Trials p. 283, *see generally, Note, The Responsibility of Employers For the Action of Their Employees: The Negligent Hiring Theory of Liability*, 53 Chi-Kent L. Rev. 717 [1976]).

Calvosa asks that any judgment rendered against him in favor of Vincenzino be apportioned between Calvosa and the third-party defendant and/or that the third-party defendant is bound to indemnify him for any recovery by Vincenzino.

The issue presented is whether the alleged negligent hiring of plaintiff by NYSA-ILA Medical Center may be interposed as a third-party complaint under these circumstances.

The codification of *Dole v. Dow Chemical Co.*, 30 NY2d 143, 331 NYS2d 382, is embodied in CPLR Article 14. This statute applies not only to joint tortfeasors, but also to concurrent, successive, independent and even intentional tortfeasors. (*Board of Education v. Sargent Webser, Crenshaw & Folley*, 71 NY2d 21, 523 NYS2d 475, 478).

The section is not limited to unintentional tortfeasors. The Court of Appeals has suggested that no such limitation should be placed upon the expanded right to contribution "Dole now permits apportionment... regardless of the degree or nature of the concurring fault..." *(Kelly v. Long Island Lighting Co.*, 324

NYS2d 46, 31 NY2d 25, 29, 273 N.E.2d 316 (1972). That no sound policy reason exists for denying contribution among tortfeasors where one or more is charged with intentional or reckless and wanton misconduct has been argued. *(See, e.g., Leflar, Contribution and Indemnity Between Tortfeasors*, 81 U.Pa.L.Rev. 130, 139 [1932].

The fact that contribution under Section 1401 of the CPLR has not been barred where tortfeasors are charged with reckless or intentional misconduct (Murphy, *Dole v. Dow Chemical: Thoughts About the Future*, 2 J. Ins. Negligence & Compensation L. § 17, 20–21 [1972]) is suggestive of the absence of any absolute policy in New York to bar contribution when intentional misconduct is involved. The existence of a procedure in new Article 14 for apportioning liability on the basis of relative degrees of culpability permits the use of the Article where one of the tortfeasors is guilty of intentional misconduct or reckless misconduct while another is not, without fear that the intentional wrongdoer will be "rewarded" by the presence of a non-intentional wrongdoer. The decision of the Supreme Court of Wisconsin to permit comparative contribution even where one wrongdoer was charged with gross negligence is equally applicable to the situation where one tortfeasor is charged with intentional wrongdoing: "Much of what constituted gross negligence will be found to constitute a high percentage of ordinary negligence causing the harm..." (*Bielski v. Schulze*, 16 Wis. 2d 1, 114 N.W.2d 105, 113 [1962]).

(12th Ann. Report of N.Y. Jud. Conf. on CPLR, 1974 McKinney's Session Laws of N.Y., at 1805-1806).

Consequently, as a matter of procedure, there is no bar to an intentional tortfeasor seeking contribution and an apportionment of liability from a purportedly negligent tortfeasor. As a matter of substantive law, however, the claim for contribution and/or indemnification must be precluded.

This appears to be a matter of first impression, for no cases can be found on the right to seek contribution from a party charged with the negligent hiring of the plaintiff. However, the claim is substantially similar to cases wherein an infant plaintiff is injured due to the alleged negligence of defendant, who then seeks contribution from the child's parents on the theory of negligent supervision. The cases have uniformly held that such contribution claims cannot stand. *(Smith v. Sapienza*, 52 NY2d 82, 436 NYS2d 236, 238; *Madden v. County of Nassau*, 117 AD2d 717, 498, NYS2d 856, 857 (2d Dept.); *Russo v. Osofsky*, 112 AD2d 926, 492 NYS2d 623, 624 (2d Dept.). This is so because, notwithstanding the duty of a parent to supervise his or her child, the breach thereof is not actionable by the child. (*Holodook v. Spencer*, 36 NY2d 35, 45; 364 NYS2d 859; *Smith v. Sapienza, supra*).

By parallel reasoning, the breach of any duty not to negligently hire its employees cannot be actionable by the employee himself, here plaintiff Vincenzino. Thus, it follows that the defendant/third-party plaintiff possesses no Dole claim for contribution against the allegedly negligent employer who hired plaintiff (*cf., Smith v. Sapienza, supra*). A claim for contribution exists only when two or more tortfeasors share in responsibility for the same injury, in violation of duties respectively owed to the injured person (*id., citing Holodook v. Spencer, supra*). Third-party defendant medical center, owing no independent duty to plaintiff not to negligently hire him, cannot be held responsible for such via a Dole contribution claim.

A parent may be held liable to an injured person for entrusting his or her child with a "dangerous instrumentality," (*Nolechek v. Gesuale*, 46 NY2d 332, 413 NYS2d 340), but there is no allegation that the medical center negligently entrusted or gave control of any gun which the defendant Calvosa allegedly brandished upon plaintiff.

For these reasons, the motion is granted and the third-party complaint is dismissed.

Flick v. Stewart-Warner Corporation
76 NY2d 50 (1990)

Defendant is a foreign corporation not authorized to do business in the State of New York. Plaintiff, mistakenly believing that defendant was authorized to do business in the State, commenced this action pursuant to Business Corporation Law § 306 instead of Business Corporation Law § 307 which governs service on unauthorized foreign corporations. Concededly, plaintiff effected personal service on the Secretary of State at her office in Albany and thereafter defendant received a copy of the process at its office in Chicago. The question is whether under these circumstances the court acquired personal jurisdiction over defendant although plaintiff did not send a copy of the process to defendant by registered mail as required by section 307(b)(2) or file the affidavit of compliance required by section 307(c)(2). The Appellate Division concurred with Supreme Court that jurisdiction had been acquired and affirmed its denial of defendant's motion to dismiss. CPLR § 3211(a)(8). For reasons which follow, we disagree. Accordingly, there should be a reversal.

I.

Plaintiff sustained injuries when a hose, allegedly manufactured by defendant, malfunctioned. Defendant is a Virginia corporation having a principal office in Chicago, Illinois. It had not designated the Secretary of State as its agent for service of process since July 21, 1952, when it surrendered its certificate of authority to do business in the State of New York. Apparently, assuming that defendant's designation of the Secretary of State was still in effect, plaintiff served two copies of the summons with notice on the Secretary at her office in Albany pursuant to Business Corporation Law § 306. The Secretary of State's office, after signing a receipt for the process, found from its records that defendant's certificate of authority had been canceled in 1952. It nevertheless sent a copy of the process by certified mail, return receipt, to defendant at its designated address in Chicago in accordance with section 306 and thereafter got back the signed card signifying receipt of the process by defendant.

When defendant's time to answer expired, plaintiff moved for a default judgment. Defendant opposed the motion for default and filed a cross motion seeking a dismissal of the action upon the ground that the service was ineffective. It argued that the court had not acquired jurisdiction over it because plaintiff had not met the requirements of Business Corporation Law § 307 for service on an unauthorized foreign corporation in that: (1) a copy of the process was not sent "by or on behalf of the plaintiff to such foreign corporation by registered mail with return, receipt requested" as prescribed by section 307(b)(2) (instead a copy was sent by the Secretary of State by certified mail); and (2) plaintiff did not file with the clerk of the court proof of such service by registered mail in an affidavit of compliance as required by section 307(c)(2).

Although Supreme Court denied defendant's dismissal motion, it also denied plaintiff's motion for a default and ordered plaintiff to accept defendant's notice of appearance and to serve a complaint within 30 days. On defendant's appeal, the Appellate Division unanimously affirmed. That court rejected the argument that the failure to comply with section 307 was jurisdictional.

The Appellate Division noted that there was no dispute that the Secretary of State had been duly served in Albany and reasoned that since "the Secretary of State is the statutory agent for unauthorized foreign corporations (Business Corporation Law § 307[a]), this personal delivery of the summons constituted literal compliance with the jurisdictional requirements of CPLR § 311(1), which allows for personal service on a corporation by delivering the summons to an agent authorized by law to receive service" (*Flick v. Stewart-Warner*

Corp., 151 AD2d 823, 824). It concluded that plaintiff's failures of compliance with the registered mail and proof of service requirements of the statute (§ 307[b][2]; [c][2]) were "mere irregularities that * * * do not deprive the court of jurisdiction" (*id.*, at 825). The Appellate Division granted defendant leave to appeal and certified the following question: "Did this court err as a matter of law in affirming so much of the Supreme Court's order as denied defendant's motion to dismiss the summons with notice?" We now reverse and answer the certified question in the affirmative.

II.

The question is whether the procedures established in Business Corporation Law § 307 are requirements of a jurisdictional nature which must be strictly satisfied. Plaintiff's argument, adopted by the Appellate Division, is that the only jurisdictional requirement is personal service on the Secretary of State who by the terms of section 307(a) is appointed defendant's agent for service of process. Once service on the Secretary of State is complete, the argument goes, jurisdiction is acquired and subsequent deviations from required procedures (i.e., mailing by certified rather than by registered mail and not filing the affidavit of compliance) may, in the absence of prejudice, be excused as "mere irregularities." We disagree. The argument overlooks both the critical differences in the legal bases for jurisdiction over a foreign corporation, which depend upon whether the corporation is or is not authorized to do business in the State, and the distinctions in the applicable statutes that reflect these differences.

The predicate for this State's jurisdiction over an unauthorized foreign corporation is the fact that it is doing business in the State and has thus created a constructive presence over which New York courts can exert general jurisdiction (CPLR § 301; *see, Laufer v. Ostrow*, 55 NY2d 305, 309–310; *see generally*, 1 Weinstein-Korn-Miller, N.Y. Civ. Prac. L. & R., paras. 301.14, 301.16). Assuming that the predicate for general jurisdiction over an unauthorized foreign corporation exists, section 307 prescribes the method for effecting service of process.

Service may be commenced on an unauthorized foreign corporation by serving the process "upon the secretary of state as its agent" (§ 307[a]). Such process must be served personally at the office of the Secretary of State in Albany or on the deputy or an authorized agent for service (§ 307[b]). Thereafter, notice of the service and a copy of the process must either be delivered "personally without this state to such foreign corporation" in accordance with section 307(b)(1) or sent "by or on behalf of the plaintiff to such foreign corporation by registered mail with return receipt requested" in accordance with section 307(b)(2). Regardless of whether such service is effected personally (§ 307[b][1]) or by registered mail (§ 307[b][2]) an affidavit of compliance must be filed in accordance with section 307(c)(1) or section 307(c)(2) with the clerk of the court in which the action is pending within 30 days after such service. In either case service of process is not complete until "ten days after [the affidavit of compliance containing proof of service is] filed with the clerk of the court" (§ 307[c][1], [2] [emphasis added]).

In the case of an unauthorized foreign corporation—as contrasted with a domestic corporation or a foreign corporation authorized to do business in the State—the designation of the Secretary of State as its agent for service is imputed, not actual. The designation is effected by statutory edict on the theory that by doing business in the State a foreign corporation has submitted itself to the jurisdiction of our courts (*see, Revised Supp. to Fifth Interim Report to Joint Legislative Committee to Study Revision of Corporation Laws*, 1961 N.Y. Legis. Doc. No. 12, at 23–24). Because the appointment of the Secretary of State as agent is a constructive rather than an actual designation, the statute contains procedures calculated to assure that the foreign corporation, in fact, receives a copy of the process. Section 307(b) specifies that service "shall be sufficient if notice thereof and a copy of the process" [emphasis added] are either delivered personally to the foreign corporation without the State (*see*, § 307[b][1]) or sent to it by registered mail (§ 307[b][2]). The proof called for in the affidavit of compliance is that the required actual notice has been given either by personal service or by registered mail (*see*, § 307[c][1], [2]). These are not mere procedural technicalities, but measures designed to satisfy due process requirements of actual notice.

It is significant that the Legislature, as a further assurance of actual notice to the unauthorized foreign corporation, has specified that the service of process shall not be complete until "ten days after [the required affidavit of compliance is] filed with the clerk of the court" (§ 307[c][2] [emphasis added]). The Legislature in analogous statutes pertaining to service on nonresidents, it should be noted, has seen fit to impose a similar requirement of prior compliance with all statutory procedures and safeguards as a precondition for considering the service of process to be complete (*see, e.g.*, Vehicle and Traffic Law § 253 [operating automobile within the State]; and General Business Law § 250 [operating aircraft within the State]) under which nonresidents by their activities within the State are deemed to have submitted to New York jurisdiction and to have designated the Secretary of State their agent for service of process (*see*, Vehicle and Traffic Law § 253[1]; General Business Law § 250[1]).

In contrast, service of process on a foreign corporation authorized to do business in the State is simple. There are no theoretical uncertainties concerning the basis for jurisdiction since the foreign corporation is concededly doing business in the State and, indeed, has applied for authority for the express purpose of doing so (*see*, Business Corporation Law § 1304[a]). As part of its application for authority to do business, the foreign corporation must file a signed and verified designation of the Secretary of State as its agent for service of process and it must set forth the address to which the copy of any process is to be mailed (*see*, Business Corporation Law § 1304[a][6]). Because of this express designation of the Secretary of State, there can be no question that service on the Secretary of State as the foreign corporation's designated agent is the equivalent of actual service on the foreign corporation. Thus, Business Corporation Law section 306—unlike section 307—provides that "[s]ervice of process on such corporation shall be complete when the secretary of state is so served" (§ 306[b] [emphasis added]).

In sum, we hold that strict compliance with the procedures of Business Corporation Law § 307 is required to effect service on an unauthorized foreign corporation (*accord., Lansdowne Fin. Serv. v. Binladen Telecommunications Co.*, 95 AD2d 711, 712; *Meyer v. Volkswagen of Am.*, 92 AD2d 488; *see, Macchia v. Russo*, 67 NY2d 592, 595; *see also, Adirondack Tr. Lines v. Lapaglia*, 128 AD2d 228, 231; *Elliot v. James*, 97 AD2d 428). The case of *Marine Midland Realty Credit Corp. v. Welbilt Corp.* (145 AD2d 84), cited by the Appellate Division, presents the converse of the situation before us—a foreign corporation authorized to do business in the State being served with process under the more stringent procedures of section 307, rather than under section 306. The holding in Marine Midland—that personal delivery of process to the Secretary of State in Albany was sufficient for the completion of service and that the irregularities caused by proceeding under section 307 could be disregarded—highlights the crucial point. In Marine Midland, unlike the case at bar, the defendant was authorized to do business in the State and had filed an actual designation of the Secretary of State as agent for service of process (*see*, Business Corporation Law § 1304[a][6]).

The order of the Appellate Division should be reversed, with costs, defendant's motion to dismiss plaintiff's summons with notice granted and the certified question answered in the affirmative.

Order reversed.

Exercises

1. What is the purpose of the CPLR imposing time limits on the service of process on the parties?

2. Indicate several circumstances in which a person might wish to intervene in a lawsuit.

3. Discuss in detail your opinion of the effectiveness of class action lawsuits.

4. Why would a plaintiff serve a summons and notice rather than a summons and complaint? Explain.

5. Explain the difference between impleading and interpleading.

EXHIBIT

SUPREME COURT OF THE STATE OF NEW YORK
COUNTY OF NEW YORK

___________ , **Plaintiff,**	§	
	§	
V.	§	**SUMMONS**
	§	
___________ , **Defendant**	§	

To the above named defendant:

You are hereby summoned and required to serve upon plaintiff's attorney an answer to the complaint in this action within twenty days after the service of this summons, exclusive of the day of service, or within thirty days after service is complete if this summons is not personally delivered to you within the State of New York. In case of your failure to answer, judgment will be taken against you by default for the relief demanded in the complaint.

The basis of the venue designated is {specify}.

Dated: {print name}

____
Attorney for Plaintiff
Address:
Telephone Number:

EXHIBIT

SUPREME COURT OF THE STATE OF NEW YORK
COUNTY OF NEW YORK

____________ , **Plaintiff,**	§	
	§	
V.	§	**SUMMONS WITH NOTICE**
	§	
____________ , **Defendant**	§	

To the above-named defendant:

You are hereby summoned to appear in this action by serving a notice of appearance on plaintiff's attorney within twenty days after the service of this summons, exclusive of the day of service, or within thirty days after service is complete if this summons is not personally delivered to you within the State of New York.

Take notice that the object of this action and the relief sought is {specify}, and that in case of your failure to appear judgment will be taken against you by default for the sum of __________ with interest from _____________, plus the costs and disbursements of this action.

The basis of the venue designated is {specify basis}.

Dated: {Print Name}

____
Attorney for Plaintiff
Address:
Telephone Number:

Chapter Three

PLEADINGS

Introduction

The term **pleadings** refers to the various documents filed with a court incident to the commencement and furthering of a lawsuit. In order for the court to permit the parties to proceed with a civil action, it must be demonstrated that there is a **sufficiency of the pleadings** (i.e., that the complaint and answer have indicated that there is a valid cause of action that can be adjudicated by the court in which the pleadings have been filed). If the pleadings on their face do not detail sufficient facts and legal arguments to maintain a suit, the case may be dismissed at this point by motion of the parties *(see* Chapter Four).

Historically, the type of court in which a litigant filed the pleading was dependent upon the nature of the remedy the party was seeking. If the plaintiff was seeking monetary relief, known as **damages**, then the complaint had to be filed in the law division of the appropriate court. If the plaintiff was seeking nonmonetary relief (such as an injunction, rescission or reformation of a contract), then the complaint had to be filed in the court's equity division. Until the twentieth century, law and equity were divided, and the plaintiff was forced to choose the court depending upon the remedy sought; the same suit could not be maintained in both the law and equity courts. Nowadays, law and equity have been merged, and the plaintiff may seek both legal and equitable relief in the same case, and ask for such relief in the same complaint.

However, there still remains a distinction between seeking legal or equitable relief. Jury trials are permitted only for parties seeking monetary remedies; if the remedy sought is equitable, then the matter must be decided by the judge. If the complaint filed with the court seeks both damages and equitable relief, pursuant to section 4102(c) of the CPLR, no jury is permitted. A plaintiff is prohibited from alleging monetary damages merely to seek a jury trial if none is warranted or seeking only equitable relief just to prevent the defendant from having a jury resolve the matter. In addition, if the plaintiff underestimated the amount of damages suffered when filing the complaint, under the concept of ***ad damnum***, the party may seek leave to modify the amount of damages sought at any time.

The preceding chapter discussed the procedure for making sure the pleadings are properly served on the parties. This chapter shall focus on how to create the appropriate initial pleadings to institute a lawsuit. For the paralegal, this understanding of how to draft initial pleadings is paramount to the effective fulfillment of his or her function in the law office. Paralegals are typically called upon to draft these initial documents for the attorney based on the information that has been obtained from the client through client interviews. If the pleadings are deemed defective, the lawsuit may be dismissed. Competent draftsmanship is therefore a mandatory job skill for the modern litigation paralegal.

Complaint

New York permits a lawsuit to be initiated with the filing of a simple summons and notice with the clerk of the court; however, the defendant, if served with only a notice of the proceeding, may make a demand for the complaint that will then have to be filed and served separately. As a general rule of practice, a lawsuit is typically initiated by the filing of a summons and complaint unless the Statute of Limitations is about to expire and time constraints prohibit drafting a complete complaint in sufficient time. However, the complaint will have to be drafted and filed eventually, and it is the document that actually indicates the basis for the lawsuit. The summons and notice are forms that can be easily completed *(see* Exhibits). Note that CPLR § 2101(a) requires the summons to be typed with no less than a 12-point typeface.

The complaint is usually divided into the following sections.

- *Caption*. The caption is the heading of the complaint, indicating the court in which the complaint is being filed, the name of the parties, the title of the action, and the index number that has been purchased from the clerk of the court, which is used for filing and identification purposes.

  Example:

  STATE OF NEW YORK
  SUPREME COURT, COUNTY OF MONROE

John Jones, an Individual,	§	
Plaintiff,	§	*Breach of Contract*
V.	§	
Marian Mills, an Individual,	§	
Defendant	§	*Index No. __________*

  COMPLAINT

In the caption, or heading, of the complaint, the legal status of the parties must be indicated: an individual, a corporation, an infant, and the like. Note that after the caption each paragraph of the complaint should be individually numbered.

- *Allegation of Jurisdiction*. The first section of the body of the complaint alleges the jurisdiction of the court. New York permits such allegations of jurisdiction to be omitted, but a well-drafted complaint should still specify the jurisdiction to minimize challenges later. Furthermore, if the matter is brought in a federal court, the allegation of jurisdiction is always included.

  Example: This Court has jurisdiction over this matter because the defendant is a domestic corporation and regularly transacts business in the state of New York. The amount in controversy exceeds the jurisdictional minimum for this Court.

- Statement of Facts. The statement of facts indicates the basis upon which the lawsuit is being brought. It may be necessary to attach to the complaint documentary evidence relating to the facts alleged.

  Example: *On or about July 1, 1998, defendant and plaintiff entered into a contract for the lease of five motor vehicles for a period of three years at an annual rental for each vehicle of $10,000. See attached Lease Agreement.*

- Cause of Action. The cause of action specifies the legal wrong that the plaintiff is claiming that she or he has suffered based on the factual allegations. A plaintiff is permitted to plead as many causes of action as may be appropriate to the situation, and may allege inconsistent causes, such as suing for breach of contract and promissory estoppel arising out of the same facts. Remember, the cause of action is important because it provides the legal basis for the lawsuit—if no cause of action is alleged, the suit may be dismissed. Each cause of action must be listed separately in separate paragraphs.

- Prayer for Relief. The complaint's Prayer for Relief indicates the remedies that the plaintiff is seeking. For damages, general and special damages are requested separately, and the prayer may also seek attorney's fees and court costs, as well as a prayer for equitable relief.

  Example: *Prayer for Relief*
  Plaintiff prays for:
  1. *$27,500 in compensatory damages*
  2. *Attorney's fees*
  3. *Court Costs.*

- *Signature*. The plaintiff, or the plaintiff's agent, must sign the complaint.

- *Verification*. A **verification**, which will be discussed in detail below, is a statement under oath confirming the truth of the allegations contained in the pleadings.

The CPLR sets out certain rules with respect to creating a complaint for particular kinds of lawsuits.

- For contracts, the plaintiff need not plead conditions precedent. CPLR § 3015(a).
- For corporations, the corporate state must be specifically stated. CPLR § 3015(h).
- For negotiable instruments, a specific denial of a signature is necessary. CPLR § 3015(d).
- Specificity in the allegation is required for the following types of actions:
  1. defamation
  2. fraud
  3. misconduct in a divorce or separation action
  4. satisfaction of a judgment
  5. alleging the laws of a foreign country
  6. itemized accounts
  7. no-fault automobile accident
  8. existence of a license
  9. prayer for relief in a medical malpractice case
  10. certificate of an expert in a medical malpractice case.

"Specificity" means that the details giving rise to these actions must be explicitly given. For all other actions, the complaint may allege the causes of action in general terms.

Example: Defendant was licensed to practice medicine in this state on May 31, 1990, by the New York Department of Education, as evidenced by the attached certificate issued by said Department.

Example: On or about August 3, 1999, defendant did willfully, wantonly and recklessly drive his car into the plaintiff at the intersection of Broadway and 23d Street in the city of New York.

Answer and Reply

As indicated in the preceding chapter, every complaint requires an answer by the defendant, and every counterclaim asserted by a defendant in an answer requires a reply from the plaintiff. The form of the answer and reply mirror the format of the complaint: caption, index number, heading (Answer or Reply), body in which the allegations are admitted or denied, any counterclaims asserted, prayer for relief, signature, and verification. However, because these pleadings are responsive, the defendant in the answer, and the plaintiff in the reply, must address each allegation stated by the opposing party.

The defendant in the answer may either admit or deny the plaintiff's allegations. Some allegations are easily admitted, such as a name, address, and so forth. Denial may take one of several forms.

- *Specific denial*. This is used when the defendant denies a particular allegation in the complaint.

  Example: Defendant specifically denies the allegations contained in Paragraphs 7-10 of the Plaintiff's complaint.

- *General denial*. This is the form generally used in which the defendant makes a broad statement denying the allegations stated in the complaint.

  Example: Defendant denies all of the allegations contained in Plaintiff's first cause of action.

- *Denial based on information and belief*. When the defendant has no specific facts to corroborate his or her denial but believes the allegations are incorrect, this answer may be used.

> <u>Example</u>: *Based on Defendant's information and belief he can neither admit nor deny the allegations contained in Paragraph 3 of the Complaint.*

Anything not denied in a responsive pleading is deemed to be admitted and, when no further pleadings are required, all allegations in the last permitted pleading are deemed denied by the party opposing the pleading. CPLR § 3018(a).

After responding to the specific paragraphs of the complaint, the defendant may assert any affirmative defense he or she may have to the action. An **affirmative defense** is the legal basis whereby the defendant asserts that he or she is not liable to the plaintiff. Affirmative defenses may take the form of an alibi ("I was not in New York at the time in question.") or any legal claim for non-liability (previous payment, accord and satisfaction, Statute of Frauds, etc.). Affirmative defenses appear in section 3211 of the CPLR.

<u>Example</u>: *Defendant states that she is not liable to the plaintiff because the defendant has already paid the plaintiff the amount in question.*

The defendant in a civil lawsuit is permitted, in the answer, to assert any counterclaim he or she may have against the plaintiff. A **counterclaim** is the assertion of a cause of action by the defendant against the plaintiff. The common law recognizes two forms of counterclaims: compulsory and permissive. A **compulsory counterclaim** is a cause of action arising out of the same set of circumstances involving the same parties; if a compulsory counterclaim is not raised it is deemed waived. A **permissive counterclaim** is a cause of action the defendant has against the plaintiff not arising out of the same circumstances that gave rise to the present action. A permissive counterclaim may, but need not, be raised in the answer; it may form the basis of its own suit later. New York makes no distinction between permissive and compulsory counterclaims.

<u>Example</u>: *The plaintiff and defendant were the drivers in a car accident. The plaintiff is alleging serious injuries resulting from the*

defendant's negligent driving. The defendant also suffered injuries, and claims that the accident was the plaintiff's fault. The defendant must also assert her claim for injuries against the plaintiff in her answer.

Example: The same litigants from the above example have knowledge of each other and have business dealings together. The defendant believes that plaintiff has breached a contact that they have entered into. The defendant may assert his permissive counterclaim in her answer.

In the answer, a defendant may also assert any claim he or she may have against a codefendant, known as **cross-claim**. CPLR § 3019(b). If any counterclaim or cross-claim has been filed, the plaintiff and or codefendant must answer such allegations in a **reply** that follows the same format as the answer already discussed.

Verification

As stated above, a verification is a statement under oath that certifies the truth of the allegations contained in the pleadings. CPLR § 3020–3023. If the party making the verification will not take an oath because of religious or moral reasons, the verification may be made by affirmation before a notary public.

The party to the action should make the verification, but the party's attorney may verify the pleading upon a showing why the party was unable to do so. If the litigant is a domestic (i.e., New York) corporation, an officer of the corporation makes the verification; foreign corporations (i.e., those organized under the laws of a state other than New York) may have their pleadings verified by their attorneys. The verification states that the statements contained in the pleadings are true based on the personal knowledge and belief of the party taking the oath. Verification for complaints is optional except in

- actions against co-obligors (CPLR § 1502)
- actions for goods sold or services rendered (CPLR § 3016[b])
- Article 78 proceedings
- matrimonial actions except for allegations of adultery.

If the complaint is verified, the subsequent pleading must also be verified. Regardless of whether the complaint was verified, the following responses must be verified:

- answer that alleges fraud or fraudulent conveyance
- dilatory defense
- action against a corporation on a promissory note.

Anytime an infant is a party to the action, the pleading must be verified. Also, a Bill of Particulars must be verified if

- the pleading was verified
- the action is for negligence (CPLR § 3044).

If the pleading is required to be verified and it is not, the pleading may be considered as a nullity.

Bill of Particulars

The function of a **bill of particulars** is to reduce the issues that must be litigated at trial. The party who has the burden of proof with respect to a particular issue is the party who is entitled to make the demand on the opposing side to streamline the litigation process. A party may not serve the opposing side with both a Bill of Particulars and written interrogatories *(see* Chapter Four) without leave of the court. A Bill of Particulars is a form of discovery used in the New York courts to expedite the litigation process and to promote the settlement of disputes before trial.

Procedure

The party with the burden of proof serves the opposing party with the Bill of Particulars. The opposing side must respond within 30 days of the service.

The form for the Bill of Particulars is not set out in the CPLR, but if the party responding to the Bill of Particulars wishes to object to a question, the objection must be raised before or with the answer. If the party who must respond fails to respond, the party seeking the response may seek an Order to Compel an answer from the court *(see* Chapter Four). The court has the power to compel answering, or it might modify the bill if the questions are deemed improper or place an undue burden on the responding party.

If special damages are claimed, a supplemental Bill of Particulars may be served not less than 30 days before the trial date without leave of court; otherwise, supplemental Bills of Particulars are only permitted with court approval. Once the Bill of Particulars has been served, the opposing party may begin discovery upon seven days notice to the demanding party. CPLR § 3043. Bills of Particulars are devices required under New York law—discovery itself will be discussed in detail in the next chapter.

Interlocutory Papers

All litigation papers other than those served with the initial summons are deemed to be interlocutory. Service of process for initial pleadings was discussed in Chapter Two. The following rules apply to serving interlocutory papers:

- Personal service is always permitted and is generally favored.
- When using ordinary mail, the envelope must be stamped, addressed, and mailed. Five days are added to the time to reply if ordinary mail is used (not for service of process).
- With consent of the opposing party, service may be affected by facsimile, but the servicing party also must mail a confirmation letter.
- Overnight delivery is permitted; however, if this method is used, the responding party is entitled to one additional day in which to reply.

<u>Example</u>: *The plaintiff in a lawsuit sends the Bill of Particulars to the defendant by ordinary mail. The defendant now has 35*

days in which to respond (30 days plus five additional days because of ordinary mail).

Ethical Concerns

Many times attorneys will avoid serving the defendant with a complaint simply to drag out the litigation process and to force additional work on the defendant—that is, the defendant is forced to demand a copy of the complaint. Although serving a summons and notice are legally permitted, they are generally disfavored and raise certain questions with respect to the tactics employed by the plaintiff's counsel.

Chapter Review

The summons and notice—or complaint—are the initial papers used to initiate a lawsuit. Paralegals are typically called upon to draft the initial pleadings if the client is the plaintiff, and to assist the attorney in drafting the answer for the defendant, as well as any replies that might be required.

The format of the complaint is fairly straightforward.

- Caption with Index Number
- Title
- Allegation of Jurisdiction
- Statement of Facts
- Cause of Action
- Prayer for Relief
- Signature
- Verification

The defendant's answer should either admit or deny the allegations specified in the complaint, and the defendant must assert any appropriate affirmative defense. Furthermore, the defendant in the answer should assert any counterclaim the defendant has against the plaintiff, as well as any cross-claim he or she may have against the codefendants.

Once the answer and any replies have been served, the party with the burden of proof may begin discovery by serving a Bill of Particulars on the opposing party to minimize litigable issues. Once the Bill of Particulars has been served, the opposing party may begin discovery within seven days of notifying the other party of his or her intention to do so.

Key Terms

Affirmative defense – legal basis asserted by the defendant to disclaim liability

Answer – a defendant's reply to the complaint

Bill of Particulars – the initial written questions demanded by the party with the burden of proof to resolve litigable issues

Caption – the heading of the pleadings

Cause of action – the legal basis for the lawsuit

Complaint – the document filed by the plaintiff that indicates the factual and legal basis of the lawsuit

Compulsory counterclaim – a counterclaim arising out of the same transaction between the same parties as in the initial lawsuit; must be asserted or is deemed waived

Counterclaim – a cause of action the defendant may have against the plaintiff

Damages – monetary relief

Denial based on knowledge and belief – form of denial used when defendant does not have specific facts to make a specific denial

General denial – denying of all of the allegations

Interlocutory papers – all documents other than the initial summons and notice or complaint

Permissive counterclaim – a counterclaim not arising out of the same transaction as the current lawsuit that may be asserted in the answer

Pleadings – papers filed with the court incident to a lawsuit

Prayer for relief – section of a complaint in which the plaintiff asks for remedies

Reply – responsive pleading answering a counterclaim

Specific denial – denial of a particular allegation

Sufficiency of the pleadings – requirement that the pleadings be complete enough to indicate a cause of action

Verification – statement under oath certifying the truth of the matters appearing in the pleadings

Edited Judicial Decisions

Oceana Apts. v. Spielman
164 Misc. 2d 98, 623 NYS2d 724 (Civ. 1995)

Motion to dismiss denied at this time. Petitioner may make written application by motion to amend verification. Thirty-dollar costs awarded to respondent.

I.
CLAIM FOR DISMISSAL

The respondent moves to dismiss the petition for the following reasons:

1. The petition fails to have annexed to it the registration statement.
2. The verification in the petition fails to meet the requirements of CPLR § 3021 in that the attorney verification failed to state why the petitioner did not make the verification.

The petitioner admits the registration omissions brought out by the respondent but argues that such an omission should not result in a dismissal of the petition. The petitioner argues further that the verification is proper and if found to be improper was waived by the respondent because it was raised late.

II.
FAILURE TO ANNEX THE REGISTRATION STATEMENT

Section 27-2107(b) of the Housing Maintenance Code (Administrative Code of City of N.Y., tit. 27, ch. 2) makes the requirements about registration clear:

> In any action to recover possession under section seven hundred eleven of the real property actions and proceedings law, the owner shall set forth his or her registration number issued by the department, and shall allege that he has filed a statement of registration and shall annex a copy of the receipt of such registration to his or her petition.

The Housing Maintenance Code therefore requires petitioner to do the following in summary proceedings:

1. Set forth the registration number issued by the Department of Housing Preservation and Development,
2. Allege that a registration statement has been filed, and
3. Annex a copy of the registration receipt to the petition.

In the instant proceeding, the petitioner has provided the multiple dwelling registration number, and stated that there is a currently effective registration statement on file, but it has failed to attach a copy of the registration receipt as the Code requires.

The petitioner therefore has failed to comply with the requirements of section 27-2107(b) of the Housing Maintenance Code. The respondent therefore seeks the petition to be dismissed. The respondent cites a number of cases, but none that mandate a dismissal for failure to annex a registration receipt to the petition. The court notes that the Court of Appeals case cited by the respondent has nothing to do with a failure to annex the required registration receipt. (*See*, *Matter of Blackgold Realty Corp.* v. *Milne*, 69 NY2d 719 [1987].) This court found no cases that hold that the failure to annex the registration receipt as is required under the law constitutes a substantial defect that is sufficiently prejudicial to merit or mandate a dismissal of the petition.

Rather, this court believes it represents the kind of error that the appellate courts would find to be minor, nonprejudicial, and therefore correctable. (*See*, *150 W. 26th St. Corp. v. Hall*, NYLJ, Jan. 12, 1982, at 11, col. 1 [App. Term, 1st Dept.]; *Phillips v. Mason*, NYLJ, June 29, 1982, at 5, col. 1 [App. Term, 1st Dept.]; *Jackson v. New York City Hous. Auth.*, 88 Misc. 2d 121 [App. Term, 1st Dept. 1976].)

III.
INSUFFICIENT VERIFICATION AND WAIVER

A. REQUIREMENTS OF THE LAW

RPAPL § 741 permits verification by an attorney pursuant to subdivision (d) of CPLR § 3020. It also states that an attorney may verify the petition on information and belief even if the person is in the county where the attorney has his office.

CPLR § 3020(d)(3) provides that the verification of a pleading shall be made by the affidavit of the party, except

1. if the party is not in the county where the attorney has his office
2. if the action is founded upon a written instrument for the payment of money only which is in the possession of an agent or the attorney
3. if all the material allegations of the pleading are within the personal knowledge of the attorney, the verification may be made by the attorney.

CPLR § 3021 sets forth the required form of the affidavit of verification as follows:

1. It must indicate that the pleading is true to the knowledge of the deponent, except as to matters stated to be on information and belief.
2. With regard to those matters alleged to have been stated on information and belief, he believes it to be true.
3. If the verification is made by a person other than the party, he or she must indicate in the affidavit of verification the grounds of his belief as to all matters not stated upon his knowledge.
4. The deponent must also state the reason why the party does not make the verification.

CPLR § 3022 prescribes the remedy for defective verification. It indicates that a defectively verified pleading shall be treated as a nullity provided the recipient gives notice to the adverse party's attorney with due diligence. The courts have defined due diligence to be within 24 hours after receipt of the pleading. (*See*, *State of New York v. McMahon,* 78 Misc. 2d 388 [Sup. Ct. 1974]; *Matter of Lentlie v. Egan*, 94 AD2d 839 [3d Dept. 1983], *aff'd.* 61 NY2d 874 [1984].)

B. APPLICATION OF THE LAW

1. The Verification

The pleading in the instant case contains the following omission: the verification fails to indicate why the party did not make the verification.

2. The Waiver of the Defense

Accordingly, the respondent seeks the dismissal of the petition. The petitioner counters that the respondent took six weeks to make his motion to dismiss. He argues that this is substantially beyond the due diligence requirement and therefore constitutes waiver of the defense.

In view of the fact that the respondent appeared *pro se* and only very recently retained an attorney who raised the matter at his first appearance in this summary proceeding, the court refuses to find that the defense of improper verification has been waived.

3. Is the Incomplete Verification Fatal?

The respondent claims the omission of a required element in the verification mandates that the petition be dismissed.

The courts require that before a dismissal is warranted, the defective pleadings must be consequential and prejudicial. The courts generally refuse to deny jurisdiction simply because of defective pleadings. Therefore, unless a verification defect has been shown to be substantially prejudicial, petitions are amendable. (*See*, *Hablin Realty Corp. v. McCain*, 123 Misc. 2d 777 [App. Term, 1st Dept. 1984]; 3 Weinstein-Korn-Miller, N.Y. Civ. Prac. P. § 3022.04, at 30-526–30-527; *City of New York v. Brown*, 119 Misc. 2d 1054 [Civ. Ct. 1982].) Accordingly, this court finds that the defective verification does not constitute a sufficient basis for dismissal.

C. ORDERS OF THE COURT

Therefore the court will permit the petitioner to make a motion to amend the verification by making such a motion in writing and outlining the change to be proposed in the verification in the pleading: that is, why the verification was not made by the party. The petitioner, however, since he is required to prove registration in putting forth his *prima facie* case need not move to amend the petition except to conform to the evidence shown if it sustains his *prima facie* case.

The court however awards the respondent $30 costs because the defect in the verification is required by law and the petitioner would have easily averted this controversy by pleading in conformity with the CPLR and RPAPL by providing the parties and the court with a complete verification.

Exercises

1. Go to the library and find three sample forms for a complaint.

2. Go to the library and find three sample forms for an answer.

3. Under what circumstances would a defendant be wise to assert a permissive counterclaim? Explain.

4. What is the purpose of having pleadings verified? Discuss.

5. Why may interlocutory papers be sent in a less formal manner than the initial pleadings? Explain.

Exhibit

SUPREME COURT OF THE STATE OF NEW YORK
COUNTY OF NEW YORK

___________ , **Plaintiff,**	§	
	§	**Complaint**
V.	§	
	§	**Index No.** _________
___________ , **Defendant**	§	

1. On January 1, 2000, on a public highway called Lexington Avenue in New York City, defendant ____________, negligently drove a motor vehicle against plaintiff who was then crossing this highway.
2. That motor vehicle was then owned by defendant ______________ and driven by defendant.
3. Solely as a result of defendant ___________'s negligence, plaintiff was personally injured, lost earnings and incurred expenses for {specify}.

Wherefore plaintiff demands judgment against ______________ for the sum of $_____________, and costs and disbursements.

Dated: {Print name}

____
Attorney for plaintiff
Address:
Telephone Number:

Exhibit

VERIFICATION

STATE OF NEW YORK §
CITY OF BUFFALO §
COUNTY OF ERIE §

______________________, being duly sworn, states that she is the plaintiff in this action and that the foregoing complaint is true to her own knowledge, except as to matters therein stated to be alleged on information and belief and as to those matters she believes to be true.

Dated:________________ ________________________

{Print Name}

Exhibit

Answer to Complaint, Counterclaim and Cross-Claim

SUPREME COURT OF THE STATE OF NEW YORK
COUNTY OF QUEENS

X, Plaintiff,	§	
	§	**Answer**
V.	§	
	§	**Index No. __________**
Y and Z, Defendants	§	

1. Defendant Y admits the allegations in paragraphs 1 and 4 of the complaint; states that he lacks knowledge or information sufficient to form a belief as to the truth of the allegations in paragraphs 2 and 3 of the complaint; and denies each and every other allegation in the complaint.

First Affirmative Defense

2. The cause of action set forth in the complaint did not accrue within six years next before the commencement of this action.

Second Affirmative Defense

3. Defendant Y entered into the contract annexed to the complaint as Exhibit A in reliance upon the truth of the oral statements made by plaintiff to defendant on or about May 1, _____, the {specify the alleged misrepresentation}.

4. Plaintiff made those statements to induce defendant Y to enter into the contract and with the intention that defendant Y rely upon the plaintiff's statements.

5. In fact and to the knowledge of plaintiff at the time she made those statements, they were false in that {state facts}.

Counterclaim

{Set forth any cause of action as a counterclaim in the manner in which a claim is pleaded in a complaint here.}

Cross-Claim Against Defendant Z

{Set forth any cause of action as a cross-claim against defendant Z in the manner in which a claim is pleaded in a complaint here.}

Wherefore defendant Y demands judgment (1) against plaintiff dismissing the complaint, (2) against plaintiff on the counterclaim in the sum of $_______________ plus interest, (3) against defendant Z on the cross-claim in the sum of $__________________ plus interest, and (4) against plaintiff and defendant Z for costs and disbursements.

Dated: _______________ {Print Name}

____
Attorney for Defendant Y
Address:
Telephone Number:

Chapter Four

MOTION PRACTICE

Introduction

A motion is a request by a litigant to the court asking the court to take some action. Motions are typically used to speed up the judicial process by having the court order a party to a lawsuit to comply with some request.

Generally, motions fall into two categories: *ex parte* motions and motions on notice. An ***ex parte* motion** is a motion made by one party to the court in which the opposing side is not required to be notified of the motion. There are three types of *ex parte* motions.

1. *Motion for Expedited Service*. As discussed in Chapter One, if the other methods of service of process have been tried and have failed, a party may ask leave of the court to use a different method of service to notify the defendant that a lawsuit has been initiated. Because the purpose of this motion is to notify the opposing side of a pending lawsuit, the opposing side does not come to court to respond to the motion. CPLR § 308(5).
2. *Motion for Service by Publication*. As with expedited service, if the plaintiff is seeking to effect service of process by publication because the other methods of service of process have proved to be ineffective, the motion may be made orally to the court *ex parte*. (CPLR § 315).
3. *Motion for an Order of Attachment or for a Temporary Restraining Order (TRO)*. These two provisional remedies, which will be discussed in detail below, require immediate orders to protect the alleged rights of the plaintiff. If time were permitted to notify the defendant, the plaintiff's rights might be lost, and so for this reason *ex parte* motions are permitted.

All other motions made to the court must be made with notice to the opposing party, who is afforded the opportunity to respond in writing. With a notice motion, both sides are given the opportunity to present oral argument to the court.

Paralegals play a vital role in motion practice. The paralegal will do some of the legal research to determine the legality of the motion requested, will draft the initial motion or response and order for the court, will assist in preparing a memorandum of law for presentation to the court, and may accompany the attorney to court for the hearing. Also, the paralegal is usually responsible for seeing that the opposing side is notified of all notice motions.

Procedure

Ex Parte Motions

The venue for an *ex parte* motion is anywhere in the state. As can be seen from the above introduction, *ex parte* motions are made before the opposing side has been notified of the lawsuit and, for the provisional remedies, may even be made before the plaintiff has filed the initial pleading (*see below*). When the motion is filed the moving party must attach "papers" to the motion, primarily an affidavit in support of the action requested by the motion. The affidavits are designed to demonstrate the moving party's right to the relief sought, and must indicate the status of any prior motion made for the same requested relief. The motion is deemed made when it is submitted to the court.

Motions on Notice

Motions on notice are initiated once an action has been commenced and so the appropriate court for filing the motion is the court in which the action is being tried. In addition to the motion and attached papers necessary for *ex parte* motions, for a motion on notice the moving party must also include the specific place, date, time of the hearing, plus indicate the relief requested and the grounds upon which the moving party believes the relief should be granted. The date specified for the hearing on the motion is referred to as the **return date**.

The motion must be served on the opposing party at least eight days before the return date. The opposing party is usually served by mail, but can be notified by fax (five days must be added for mailed service). If the notice is served by overnight mail, the return date must be at least nine days after such mailing.

The opposing party may respond to the motion, and the response must be sent at least two days before the hearing date. If the hearing date is between 12 and 17 days after the service, the responding party must answer no less than seven days before the hearing date. If a response is made, the moving party may reply at least one day before the hearing. Furthermore, the responding party may answer with a cross-motion against the moving party.

At the hearing both sides may present their arguments. If the court believes that the motion raises a triable issue of fact, the court may order an immediate bench trial to determine these issues before ruling on the motion. Also, a party may request an adjournment of the hearing which the court may grant. A litigant may request up to three adjournments for a total of 60 days pursuant to Uniform Rule 202.8.

Example: *The defendant in a lawsuit moves to have the action dismissed for lack of personal jurisdiction. The defendant files a motion with the court along with affidavits to support her position. The motion is filed with the court on October 1, and specifies a return date of October 15. The defendant sends notice of the motion to the plaintiff on October 2–13 days before the return date. The plaintiff responds by sending the response to the defendant by fax on October 8 (seven days before the hearing). At the hearing, the judge determines that there is a triable issue of fact as to whether the defendant resides in New York, and has a bench trial to determine that issue before ruling on the motion.*

If one of the parties so wishes, he or she may require an **order to show cause** to accelerate the hearing date.

<u>Example</u>: *The moving party specifies a return date 30 days after the date of filing the motion. The opposing party files a motion to show cause to have the hearing date moved up so that the matter may be settled quickly.*

Appeals

Ex parte motions are not appealable, and the moving party must adhere to the court's denial of the action. Motions on notice may be appealed by the losing party to the Appellate Division except for the following:

- motions made pursuant to Article 78 proceedings
- motions for a more definite statement
- motions denied because they contain scandalous matters.

A losing party may also make a **motion to review** if new facts have come to light, which is appealable. However, the denial of a **motion for reargument** is not appealable.

<u>Example</u>: *After her motion to dismiss the action was denied, the defendant moves for a reargument to provide the court with additional legal precedent to support her claim. The court denies the motion, and the defendant may not appeal the denial. This motion was based on a desire to present new legal arguments, not based on new facts being discovered.*

Types of Motions

Motions generally fall into the following four broad categories:

Motions Dealing With the Pleadings

- A **motion for a more definite statement** is used to compel the litigants to be more precise in the nature of the cause of action and the factual allegations in the pleadings.
- A **motion to strike** unnecessary, scandalous, or prejudicial matter is used to delete scurrilous matters from the pleading (not used for defamation if the matters are the defamatory statements) in order to preserve the dignity of the judicial process.
- A motion that the pleading's allegations be separately stated or numbered is used to make the pleadings more readily comprehensible; generally, a motion to make the pleadings more organized.

Regulatory Motions

- A **motion to change venue** is used to move the location of the courthouse (as discussed in Chapter One).
- A **motion to consolidate or sever** is used to make the judicial process more efficient by joining separate actions that should be heard together or separating actions that should be heard on their own. CPLR § 602, 603.
- A **motion for a separate trial** is used if there are multiple parties who believe that due process requires that their defenses be individually evaluated.

Motions to Amend the Pleadings

A party is free to amend his or her pleadings once without leave of the court or the opposing side. A party may amend the pleadings to conform the pleadings to additionally discovered facts or to add or delete causes of action. The amendment may be made without motion if

1. more than 20 days have elapsed after filing the original action,
2. the time to reply to the pleading has not expired, or

3. within 20 days after service of a pleading that responds to the original pleading.

A litigant is only permitted one "free" amendment; after that, all other amendments can be made only with leave of the court by motion or by agreement (**stipulation**) of the opposing party. Also, the court can permit the original pleadings to be amended to conform to the evidence either before or after a judgment has been rendered.

Dispositive Motions

Dispositive motions are used to terminate the litigation process.

Motion to Dismiss

A **motion to dismiss** can be made only once before a responsive pleading is required to be served. CPLR § 3211. The elements that may be used to support this motion are

1. documentary evidence
2. lack of subject matter jurisdiction
3. lack of capacity of the party
4. another action pending in another court on the same cause of action
5. affirmative defenses:
   a. arbitration
   b. collateral estoppel or res judicata
   c. discharge in bankruptcy
   d. disability of the moving party
   e. payment
   f. release
   g. Statute of Limitations
   h. Statute of Frauds
6. counterclaim not properly asserted
7. failure to state a cause of action for which relief may be granted (**demurrer**)

8. lack of personal jurisdiction
9. absence of a mandatory party to the lawsuit.

Although a motion to dismiss is usually made by the defendant, a plaintiff can also make such a motion to dismiss a particular defense raised by the defendant in his or her answer. If a party fails to move to dismiss based on a jurisdictional claim (except for subject matter jurisdiction) the jurisdictional defense is deemed waived.

In addition to the litigants' motions to dismiss, the court, on its own initiative (*sua sponte*), may dismiss a suit for any of the following reasons:

- lack of subject matter jurisdiction
- failure to state a cause of action
- lack of an indispensable party.

Orders resulting from a motion to dismiss are appealable.

Motion for Summary Judgment

A **motion for summary judgment** can be made at any time after the answer or reply has been filed, but must be made within 120 days after a motion to dismiss has been made. A motion for summary judgment requests the court to resolve the matter in favor of the moving party because there is no material issue of law or fact in dispute. The burden is on the moving party, and in reaching a decision the judge must consider the facts and law in a light most favorable to the nonmoving party. However, if it is determined that there is *any* issue of law or fact still in dispute, the motion may not be granted. Motions for summary judgment are often made but rarely granted.

The motion must be made with an affidavit in support attached to it. If the only issue is the amount of damages, the court might order a trial just on that issue. Furthermore, the court, on its own initiative, may grant a summary judgment in favor of the nonmoving party and a partial summary judgment may be granted with respect to certain of the issues, leaving the remaining issues for trial.

If the motion is made by the defendant, the defendant must first file his or her pleading with the court, but the court may treat a motion to dismiss for failure to state a claim upon which relief may be granted (demurrer) as a motion for summary judgment.

Once the motion is made, a hearing on the matter is set for 20 days after personal delivery of notice of the motion if made within the state of New York, or within 30 days of service. The opposing party may respond to the motion no less than ten days before the hearing date.

If the basis of the plaintiff's claim is an "instrument for payment of money only," based on a prior judgment, the plaintiff can serve a summons and notice of the motion on the defendant in lieu of filing a complaint. CPLR § 3213. An "instrument for payment of money only" is

- a negotiable instrument
- an unconditional guarantee
- any interest in which the right to payment is established by the paper.

An "instrument for the payment of money only" cannot be

- the repayment of an escrow account
- actions against an insurer after a judgment against the insured who did not pay
- payment under a contract term.

Provisional Remedies

New York law provides for five provisional remedies pursuant to the CPLR. A **provisional remedy** is court-ordered relief that may be granted to a party before the ultimate conclusion of the lawsuit, or even before the institution of the lawsuit, to protect the party from suffering irreparable harm. Five provisional remedies are available:

Attachment

Attachment is a demand for money judgment in any action other than a matrimonial suit. CPLR § 620. To be granted an order of attachment, the following grounds must be asserted:

- that the defendant is an unauthorized foreign corporation or a nonresident domiciliary of New York
- that the defendant is a resident or domiciliary who cannot be served personally
- that the defendant has secreted away assets
- that the action is one to enforce a foreign money judgment
- that the moving party was the victim of a felony and seeks the order to recover damages from the criminal.

In order for the court to grant an order of attachment, the property that is subject to the order must be located in New York. The property may consist of any property of the defendant's that is capable of being attached, including unconditional debts owed to the defendant.

A motion for attachment may be made either *ex parte* or on notice. If the motion is made before the service of the summons on the defendant, the moving party must serve the defendant with a summons within 60 days of granting the order of attachment. If the order is granted, the moving party must file an order confirming the attachment within ten days of levy if the grounds for the order were the defendant's nondomiciliary or nonresident status or the defendant is an unauthorized foreign corporation, or within five days for other defendants. The moving party may also obtain a Temporary Restraining Order valid for eight days in order to be able to have the property attached. The court requires a hearing on all motions on notice, motions to confirm, and motions to vacate or modify the order of attachment.

Example: *The plaintiff in a lawsuit has found out that the defendant is secreting away assets in case he loses the lawsuit. In order to protect himself, the plaintiff moves for an order of attachment on the bank accounts the defendant still has in his name in New York. The court grants the order, and the plaintiff obtains a temporary restraining* (see below) *to make sure the defendant does not remove the property before it can be attached. Three days after the order is granted the plaintiff moves to confirm the order, which is granted.*

The plaintiff in a motion for attachment must post a bond with the court for at least $500 in case he or she is unsuccessful. If the defendant successfully challenges the motion, the plaintiff might be required to reimburse the defendant the costs incurred in defending against the motion.

Preliminary Injunction

A motion for a **preliminary injunction** is available in any equitable suit in which a permanent injunction is being sought as the ultimate relief, or in any other action in which the plaintiff's interest in a specific subject matter is being threatened by the defendant's actions. CPLR § 6301. The preliminary injunction provides relief during litigation until the court renders a final decision on the matter. In order to prevail, the plaintiff must establish

- that a legal remedy (i.e., money) would be insufficient
- that he or she is likely to be entitled to the ultimate relief sought (the permanent injunction)
- that he or she has "clean hands"—is not guilty of any unethical conduct with respect to the matter
- that the injury to his or her interest is immediate and irreparable.

Before granting this provisional relief, the court may require the plaintiff to post a bond with the court to reimburse the defendant for costs if the plaintiff's claim ultimately proves to be unsuccessful. If a preliminary injunction is ordered, it is operative against all parties to the lawsuit.

Example: *The defendant has started construction of a building that the plaintiff claims will interfere with his access to the road. Rather than waiting until a complete trial on the issue, the plaintiff seeks a preliminary injunction to stop the defendant from continuing the construction.*

Briefly, a word about the relationship between a **temporary restraining order (TRO)** and a preliminary injunction: a TRO is granted *ex parte* and is used to stop an action to ensure sufficient time to have a hearing on the preliminary injunction. If the plaintiff is ultimately successful, the preliminary injunction may turn into a permanent injunction.

Receivership

Receivership is a form of provisional relief for lawsuits in which a specified piece of property is the subject matter of the action. To obtain an order of receivership, the moving party must demonstrate that there is a good chance that the property will be

- removed from New York
- sold
- materially injured
- destroyed.

An order of receivership is used when it is necessary to preserve the plaintiff's rights in the property. The person appointed to receive the property, the **receiver**, has no inherent authority; his or her authority is based on the court's order.

Example: *A woman is claiming title to a Picasso painting that her sister is currently holding in Westchester County. The sister also claims title and plans to sell the painting. The first woman moves to obtain an order of receivership to keep the property in New York until the ultimate adjudication. The receiver is ordered to take possession of the painting, to see that it is placed in a safe place, and to see that it is properly insured.*

Notice of Pendency (Lis Pendens)

A **notice of pendency** or **lis pendens** is used in actions affecting title to real property. The motion is filed with the county clerk of the county in which the real estate is located and is typically filed before the institution of the lawsuit over the realty. A party is precluded from filing a lis pendens in a summary proceeding to recover possession of real property. CPLR § 6501. The purpose of a lis pendens is to preclude anyone from affecting the title to the property until a judicial determination of the parties' rights in it.

The party who has filed the lis pendens is required to serve notice on the other parties to the potential action within 30 days of filing or the lis pendens is void. Once the lis pendens has been filed, it is effective for a period of three years but may be extended if the matter has not been settled within that time. Upon motion, for good cause, a court may extend the order.

<u>Example</u>: *A man transferred title to his house to his brother so that the brother could acquire a loan with the house as collateral. The man never intended to give up the house and has continued to reside in the house. The brother gave a mortgage on the house to a bank, but has failed to make the loan repayments and the bank is threatening to foreclose. The man files a notice of pendency with the county clerk's office to help protect his interest in the property before the bank can foreclose and sell the house at public auction.*

Replevin

Replevin is the right to possess chattel during the pendency of a lawsuit (***pendente lite***) pursuant to section 7102 of the CPLR. A motion to request replevin may be made either *ex parte* or on notice, and the party so moving must show that

- he or she is entitled to possession
- the defendant wrongfully holds the chattel
- he or she knows of no claim to the chattel or any defense thereon.

To be granted the right of replevin, the party must post a bond with the court in an amount at least equal to the value of the chattel in question. The moving party is entitled to make an *ex parte* motion if he or she can demonstrate that if the defendant received notice of the request he or she might destroy or remove the chattel. As with an order of attachment, the party must file an order to confirm within five days of the seizing of the property. The property is originally seized by the sheriff who holds the property for ten days during which time the defendant may make a motion to the court to recover the chattel.

Example: A woman claims that she loaned her pearl necklace to her friend but the friend has refused to return the necklace. The friend claims that it was a gift. The woman seeks an order of replevin to regain possession of her jewelry. She can prove to the court that the friend is planning to sell the necklace to someone who does not live in New York.

Default

A party to a lawsuit may make a **motion for default judgment** to the court requesting that the court enter a judgment in the moving party's favor because the opposing side has defaulted, (i.e., failed to respond to the litigation).

Procedure

The moving party must apply to the court for the default judgment unless the lawsuit was for a "sum certain," in which case the plaintiff may apply for the default judgment with the clerk of the court one year after the default.

Notice must be given to the defaulting party. If the defaulting party has made any appearance, he or she is entitled to at least five days notice of the application for the default judgment. If the action is against a natural person or a corporation for nonpayment of a contractual obligation, the moving party must send the defendant a copy of the motion 20 days before entry of the judgment.

A plaintiff may be susceptible to a default judgment if he or she fails to prosecute the matter. In the case of a plaintiff's default, the defendant may only seek the motion one year after the answer had been served. The plaintiff must be served by certified or registered mail within 90 days after receipt of the demand. If the plaintiff fails to show up for the trial date, the defendant must wait one year to move for the default.

Example: *The plaintiff has filed a personal injury action against the defendant who was properly served. The defendant has failed to answer the summons and complaint. The plaintiff may move the court for a default judgment in her favor, and notice must be sent to the defendant so that he can reply to the motion for the default.*

Relief from a Default Judgment

The party against whom the default judgment had been entered may move to have the judgment or order vacated within one year of the service of the judgment or order. CPLR § 5015. To have the default vacated, the defaulting party must show

- a reasonable excuse for the delay or default
- a claim or defense that has merit.

The courts have indicated that the failure of the defaulting party's attorney to answer in a timely manner may be deemed a valid excuse to vacate the default judgment. If the defendant had been personally served, the defendant may move to have the case reopened if

- less than one year has elapsed since the defendant had knowledge of the default judgment,

- less than five years have elapsed since the judgment,
- the defendant did not have personal notice of the judgment,
- the defendant has a meritorious defense.

Example: *The defendant in a lawsuit was in Europe when the suit was filed, and remained in Europe for three years. When she returned home, she discovered that she had been sued and a default judgment had been entered against her. She has reasonable grounds to have the order vacated and the case reopened.*

Ethical Concerns

Many law offices use the strategy of motion practice to undermine the opposing side's willingness to litigate. Motions can be costly and time consuming, and may be used to delay the parties from having their day in court, which is not, however, the reason why these motions were created.

The purpose of motion practice is to speed up the judicial process by giving the parties the ability to force the opposing side to address the issues by adhering to the rules and procedure of the CPLR and the courts. When used in this context motion practice furthers the efficient administration of justice. Unfortunately, motion practice may be used to thwart the judicial process and coerce a party into an unfavorable settlement simply to get the matter concluded.

Chapter Review

Motion practice is the term applied to the various requests a litigant may make to the court before the actual trial. The purpose of motion practice is to speed up the judicial process and to settle as many issues as possible before the trial.

Motions may be made *ex parte* or on notice. For motions on notice, the moving party is required to notify the opposing side of the filing of the motion. The opposing side has the opportunity to present their own arguments against the motion to the court at a hearing. After the hearing, the court issues an order either granting or denying the motion. Motions on notice may be appealed as of right to the Appellate Division except for Article 78 proceedings, motions for a more definite statement, and motions to strike scandalous matters.

Four broad categories of motions exist:

1. motions concerned with making the pleadings more articulate, understandable, or organized
2. regulatory motions that change venue, consolidate, or sever claims
3. motions to amend the pleadings
4. dispositive motions that will terminate the litigation, such as motions to dismiss, motions for summary judgment, and motions for default judgment.

In addition to these general motions, the CPLR also provides for five provisional remedies that a party can seek before an ultimate judicial decision to protect the party's rights *pendente lite*. The five provisional remedies are attachment, preliminary injunction, receivership, lis pendens, and replevin. To acquire a provisional remedy, the party must be able to demonstrate irreparable harm if the remedy is not granted, and may have to post a bond with the court.

Key Terms

Attachment – provisional remedy in which the court seizes property owned by the defendant in a suit for a money judgment

Demurrer – failure to state a claim upon which relief can be granted

Motion – request to the court

Motion for a more definite statement – request to indicate a clearer cause of action

Motion for default judgment – request to terminate the action because the other side has failed to respond

Motion for summary judgment – request to rule in the moving party's favor when there is no material issue of law or fact in dispute

Motion practice – term used to describe the various pretrial motions that are permitted

Motion to amend pleadings – request to alter the pleadings

Motion to change venue – request to move the lawsuit to another county

Motion to conform – request to change the pleadings to reflect current facts

Motion to consolidate (sever) – request to join or separate actions

Motion to dismiss – request to terminate the action

Motion to review – request to reconsider the ruling

Motion to strike – request to delete portions of the pleadings

Notice of pendency (lis pendens) – provisional remedy relating to actions over title to realty

Order to show cause – ruling to speed up the motion practice

Preliminary injunction – equitable remedy until final adjudication

Provisional remedy – relief that may be granted before the ultimate conclusion of the lawsuit

Receiver – person who holds property subject to an order of receivership

Receivership – provisional remedy to hold property

Replevin – provisional remedy to recover chattel until a judicial determination of rights

Return date – hearing date of a motion

Temporary Restraining Order (TRO) – order of court prior to the hearing on a preliminary injunction

Edited Judicial Decisions

A & M Exports, Limited v. Meridien International Bank, Ltd.
222 AD2d 378 (1st Dept. 1995)

Order of the Supreme Court, New York County (William J. Davis, J.), entered February 22, 1995, which awarded defendants judgment in the amount of plaintiff's undertaking and severed that portion of defendants' claim for attorney's fees for an assessment thereof, unanimously reversed, on the law, without costs, and the matter remanded to Supreme Court for a hearing to determine the extent of defendants' damages pursuant to CPLR § 6315.

Plaintiff commenced this action against defendants for failure to honor certain letters of credit. In connection with its application for an order of attachment pursuant to CPLR § 6201(1), plaintiff obtained a temporary restraining order (CPLR § 6210) prohibiting the transfer of $1,394,000 in assets maintained by defendants in a New York bank. However, plaintiff's complaint was ultimately dismissed on *forum non conveniens* grounds and the temporary restraining order vacated, this Court affirming (*A & M Exports v. Meridien Intl. Bank*, 207 AD2d 741, 616 NYS2d 621), without any order of attachment ever being issued. The present dispute concerns the extent of damages recoverable by defendants as a consequence of the restraint on asset transfers.

The temporary restraining order provides for an undertaking in the amount of $89,067.25 and recites that "plaintiff, if it is finally determined that it was not entitled to a temporary restraining order, will pay to the defendant [Meridien International Bank, Ltd.] and/or [Meridien Biao Bank Liberia Ltd.], all damages and costs which may be sustained by reason thereof." The undertaking itself recites that plaintiff will pay damages "not exceeding" $89,067.25. While plaintiff contends that the order and the undertaking are inconsistent, in a case involving a similar order, it was held that, absent malice, the undertaking provides the sole basis for relief. The Appellate Division, Third Department reasoned that "there is no common-law cause of action for damages sustained by an improperly procured preliminary injunction, nor does CPLR § 6315 create a statutory cause of action. The basis for damages is the undertaking itself which is a contract between the parties 'that the plaintiff, if it is finally determined that he was not entitled to an injunction, will pay to the defendant all damages and costs which may be sustained by reason of the injunction' (CPLR § 6312, subd. [b])" (*Honeywell, Inc. v. Technical Bldg. Servs.*, 103 AD2d 433, 434, 480 NYS2d 627; *RS Paralegal & Recovery Servs. v. Poughkeepsie Sav. Bank*, 190 AD2d 660, 593 NYS2d 283).

In this case, defendants moved for an order awarding damages, (1) in the amount of the undertaking pursuant to CPLR § 6212(b) and, (2) in the amount of $124,208.52, "representing costs and attorney's fees incurred in the action," pursuant to CPLR § 6212(e). In response to plaintiff's contention that the court lacked jurisdiction to entertain the application, the court deemed the motion to be brought pursuant to CPLR § 6210. As requested by defendants, the court applied the measure of damages provided in CPLR § 6212 (e), which does not limit recovery to the amount of the undertaking.

It bears emphasis that no order of attachment was ever issued in this case, and there is no basis for an award of damages premised upon the improper procurement of such an order. The temporary restraining order (TRO) provided for in CPLR § 6210 is issued pursuant to CPLR § 6313(a), and any damages sustained by reason of the operation of the order are ascertained in accordance with the provisions of CPLR § 6315, not by reference to CPLR § 6212(e) (*Salamanca Trust Co. v. McHugh,* 156 AD2d 1007, 550 NYS2d 764 [damages under CPLR § 6212(e) not recoverable unless property actually attached]; *Provisional Protective Comm. v. Williams,* 121 AD2d 271, 503 NYS2d 47 [TRO issued pursuant to CPLR § 6210 insufficient basis for award of attorney's fees pursuant to CPLR § 6212(e)]; *Augsbury v. Adams*, 108 AD2d 978, 484 NYS2d 962 [CPLR § 6212(e) damages not recoverable where application for attachment denied]).

The summary procedure of CPLR § 6315 permits the court that imposed the restraint on the transfer of a defendant's assets, which is presumably well acquainted with the dispute, to fix damages resulting from that restraint (McLaughlin, *Practice Commentaries, McKinney's Consol. Laws of N.Y.*, Book 7B, CPLR § C6315:1, at 391). "The amount of damages so ascertained is conclusive upon all persons who were served with notice of the motion and such amount may be recovered by the person entitled thereto in a separate action" (CPLR § 6315). Such an award may include counsel fees incurred in connection with an "erroneously granted temporary restraining order," where supported by the record (*Matter of Kaplan v. Werlin*, 215 AD2d 387, 388, 626 NYS2d 817, appeal dismissed 86 NY2d 868, 659 N.E.2d 763; *Watmet, Inc. v. Robinson*, 116 AD2d 998, 999, 498 NYS2d 619; *see also, Hanley v. Fox*, 90 AD2d 662, 456 NYS2d 251).

Supreme Court did not assess the extent of defendants' damages, however, but simply rendered an award for the full amount of the undertaking. While it may yet be determined that defendants' damages are in excess of the undertaking by a substantial margin, there is no statutory provision for an award of liquidated damages in the amount of the undertaking. The only evidence of record is a "billing memorandum" from counsel listing various "unbilled" fees and disbursements. In the absence of a hearing as to the propriety of counsel fees (*Morgan & Finnegan v. Howe Chem. Co.*, 210 AD2d 62, 63, 619 NYS2d 719) or any findings with respect to the nature and extent of the damages incurred by defendants, the record is insufficient to sustain the award.

A & M Exports, Limited v. Meridien International Bank, Ltd.
222 AD2d 378 (1st Dept. 1995)

Order of the Supreme Court, New York County (William J. Davis, J.), entered February 22, 1995, which awarded defendants judgment in the amount of plaintiff's undertaking and severed that portion of defendants' claim for attorney's fees for an assessment thereof, unanimously reversed, on the law, without costs, and the matter remanded to Supreme Court for a hearing to determine the extent of defendants' damages pursuant to CPLR § 6315.

Plaintiff commenced this action against defendants for failure to honor certain letters of credit. In connection with its application for an order of attachment pursuant to CPLR § 6201(1), plaintiff obtained a temporary restraining order (CPLR § 6210) prohibiting the transfer of $1,394,000 in assets maintained by defendants in a New York bank. However, plaintiff's complaint was ultimately dismissed on *forum non conveniens* grounds and the temporary restraining order vacated, this Court affirming (*A & M Exports v. Meridien Intl. Bank*, 207 AD2d 741, 616 NYS2d 621), without any order of attachment ever being issued. The present dispute concerns the extent of damages recoverable by defendants as a consequence of the restraint on asset transfers.

The temporary restraining order provides for an undertaking in the amount of $89,067.25 and recites that "plaintiff, if it is finally determined that it was not entitled to a temporary restraining order, will pay to the defendant [Meridien International Bank, Ltd.] and/or [Meridien Biao Bank Liberia Ltd.], all damages and costs which may be sustained by reason thereof." The undertaking itself recites that plaintiff will pay damages "not exceeding" $89,067.25. While plaintiff contends that the order and the undertaking are inconsistent, in a case involving a similar order, it was held that, absent malice, the undertaking provides the sole basis for relief. The Appellate Division, Third Department reasoned that "there is no common-law cause of action for damages sustained by an improperly procured preliminary injunction, nor does CPLR § 6315 create a statutory cause of action. The basis for damages is the undertaking itself which is a contract between the parties 'that the plaintiff, if it is finally determined that he was not entitled to an injunction, will pay to the defendant all damages and costs which may be sustained by reason of the injunction' (CPLR § 6312, subd. [b])" (*Honeywell, Inc. v. Technical Bldg. Servs.*, 103 AD2d 433, 434, 480 NYS2d 627; *RS Paralegal & Recovery Servs. v. Poughkeepsie Sav. Bank*, 190 AD2d 660, 593 NYS2d 283).

In this case, defendants moved for an order awarding damages, (1) in the amount of the undertaking pursuant to CPLR § 6212(b) and, (2) in the amount of $124,208.52, "representing costs and attorney's fees incurred in the action," pursuant to CPLR § 6212(e). In response to plaintiff's contention that the court lacked jurisdiction to entertain the application, the court deemed the motion to be brought pursuant to CPLR § 6210. As requested by defendants, the court applied the measure of damages provided in CPLR § 6212(e), which does not limit recovery to the amount of the undertaking.

It bears emphasis that no order of attachment was ever issued in this case, and there is no basis for an award of damages premised upon the improper procurement of such an order. The temporary restraining order (TRO) provided for in CPLR § 6210 is issued pursuant to CPLR § 6313(a), and any damages sustained by reason of the operation of the order are ascertained in accordance with the provisions of CPLR § 6315, not by reference to CPLR § 6212(e) (*Salamanca Trust Co. v.* McHugh, 156 AD2d 1007, 550 NYS2d 764 [damages under CPLR § 6212(e) not recoverable unless property actually attached]; *Provisional Protective Comm. v. Williams*, 121 AD2d 271, 503 NYS2d 47 [TRO issued pursuant to CPLR § 6210 insufficient basis for award of attorney's fees pursuant to CPLR § 6212 (e)]; *Augsbury v. Adams*, 108 AD2d 978, 484 NYS2d 962 [CPLR § 6212(e) damages not recoverable where application for attachment denied]).

The summary procedure of CPLR § 6315 permits the court that imposed the restraint on the transfer of a defendant's assets, which is presumably well acquainted with the dispute, to fix damages resulting from that restraint (McLaughlin, *Practice Commentaries, McKinney's Consol. Laws of N.Y.*, Book 7B, CPLR § C6315:1, at 391). "The amount of damages so ascertained is conclusive upon all persons who were served with notice of the motion and such amount may be recovered by the person entitled thereto in a separate action" (CPLR § 6315). Such an award may include counsel fees incurred in connection with an "erroneously granted temporary restraining order," where supported by the record (*Matter of Kaplan v. Werlin*, 215 AD2d 387, 388, 626 NYS2d 817, appeal dismissed 86 NY2d 868, 659 N.E.2d 763; *Watmet, Inc. v. Robinson*, 116 AD2d 998, 999, 498 NYS2d 619; *see also, Hanley v. Fox*, 90 AD2d 662, 456 NYS2d 251).

Supreme Court did not assess the extent of defendants' damages, however, but simply rendered an award for the full amount of the undertaking. While it may yet be determined that defendants' damages are in excess of the undertaking by a substantial margin, there is no statutory provision for an award of liquidated damages in the amount of the undertaking. The only evidence of record is a "billing memorandum" from counsel listing various "unbilled" fees and disbursements. In the absence of a hearing as to the propriety of counsel fees (*Morgan & Finnegan v. Howe Chem. Co.*, 210 AD2d 62, 63, 619 NYS2d 719) or any findings with respect to the nature and extent of the damages incurred by defendants, the record is insufficient to sustain the award.

Exercises

1. How does the procedure for an *ex parte* motion meet the requirements of due process? Explain.

2. What is your opinion of the waiting period required for the entry of a default judgment? Explain.

3. Why would a party select receivership over replevin as a provisional remedy?

4. Is there a conflict between the concept of a summary judgment and a person's right to a day in court? Explain.

5. Why would the court be concerned with deleting "scandalous" material from a pleading? Explain.

Exhibit

SUPREME COURT OF THE STATE OF NEW YORK
COUNTY OF KINGS

__________, Plaintiff	§	**Notice of Motion**
	§	**for Summary Judgment**
v.	§	**in Lieu of Complaint**
	§	
_________, Defendant	§	**Index No. ____________**

Upon the summons, dated, and the affidavit of ____________________, sworn to on ____________________, the plaintiff will move this court, at Special Term, Part 1, in Room _____, County Court House, Brooklyn, New York, on ___________________, at 9:30 a.m., for an order directing the entry of judgment for the plaintiff and against the defendant in the amount of $_____________, with interest from ______________, and for such other and further relief as to the court may seem just and proper, plus the cost of this motion, upon the ground that this action is based upon an instrument for the payment of money only which is now due and payable.

Take further notice that all answering papers shall be served on the undersigned on or before the 21st day after personal delivery of the summons to you.

Dated: ______________ {Print Name}

____
Attorney for Plaintiff
Address:
Telephone Number:

Exhibit

Notice of Motion for Protective Order on Notice to Submit to Physical Examination

Notice of Motion
{Title of court and cause}Index No.:

Please take notice that upon the annexed affidavit hereof sworn to on ______________, 2000, and the affidavit of ________________, M.D., sworn to on ________________, 2000, and upon all the pleadings and proceedings heretofore had herein, the undersigned will move this court at a {motion} term, Part ___ thereof, to be held at the courthouse thereof at __________, and __________, 2000, at ______o'clock in the afternoon of that day and as soon thereafter as counsel can be heard for an order vacating the notice to appear and submit to a physical examination heretofore served on me on the _________ day of _________, 2000, upon the grounds of physical inability to comply therewith, and for such other, further and different relief as to the court may seen just.

Yours truly,

____
Attorney for Plaintiff
Address:
Telephone Number:

Chapter Five

DISCOVERY

Introduction

The rules regarding discovery in civil proceedings are contained in Article 31 of the CPLR. The purpose of the discovery process is to provide each party to the litigation with the opportunity to ascertain the evidence the opposing side intends to present at trial so that there will be no surprise during the actual litigation. Collaterally, as the parties discover the strengths and weaknesses of each argument, they can agree either to settle the claim or at least reduce the number of issues that must be proved at trial. When the parties agree to certain points in contention, their agreement can be presented to the court as a **stipulation**, meaning that the parties have agreed to those points and they will not be contested at trial. In this manner the litigation process can be streamlined and be more cost and time efficient.

In theory, the actual discovery process begins after the plaintiff and defendant have completed the Bills of Particulars (*see* Chapter Three) and all pretrial motions not relating to the discovery process have been made and resolved. However, be aware that Bills of Particulars are in fact a discovery device, a method whereby the plaintiff and defendant can determine the strengths and weaknesses of the opponent's contentions.

According to the CPLR, all matters that are material and necessary to the prosecution or defense of the case, regardless of the burden of proof, are capable of being discovered. CPLR § 3101.These items include:

- all evidence that goes to the parties' cases in chief
- all facts that lead to the discovery of admissible evidence

- all facts, documents, and physical evidence that can be used for cross-examination.

The rules of discovery compel the following persons to submit to the discovery process:

- the parties to the action
- any predecessor in interest to the parties to the action [CPLR § 3101(a)(2)]

Example: *A landlord sold his building. A tenant is now suing the current owner of the building for violations of his lease that were originally contracted with the old owner three years before the current owner purchased the building. The original owner is subject to the discovery process because he is a predecessor in interest to the current landlord and may have evidence to support the plaintiff's case.*

- Nonparty witnesses
  1. if the witness is about to leave New York
  2. if the witness is absent from New York
  3. if the witness resides more than 100 miles from the place of trial
  4. if the witness is sick or infirm and may not be able to attend the trial

In addition
1. if expert witnesses in a medical malpractice case
2. if any other person for whom the party can convince the court of the need for discovery.

Parties to the litigation are required to submit to discovery, and only parties are subject to interrogatories (*see below*), CPLR § 3130. A court order is required for discovery from a nonparty. CPLR § 3120. Pursuant to Uniform Rule 202.12(b), discovery should be completed within twelve months for simple cases, and within fifteen months for complex ones. The courts generally discourage discovery motions and prefer the parties either to request a conference or comply with requests voluntarily.

This chapter will address the various discovery devices permitted under the CPLR, the types of information that are not discoverable, and any objections and motions that can be made with respect to the discovery process.

Privileges

Certain types of information are deemed to be **privileged** (i.e., not discoverable unless the party holding the privilege agrees to the discovery). Privileges fall into three broad categories: absolute privileges, qualified privileges, and privileges subject to special limitations.

Absolute Privileges

The CPLR recognizes two categories of absolute privileges—privileges covering information that cannot be discovered unless the person holding the privilege so agrees. The two types of absolute privileges are

- Evidence Privilege. CPLR § 3101(b). Evidentiary privileges are those specified in the rules of evidence of the state of New York. A discussion of these privileges is beyond the scope and topic of this text; however, to come within this category the privilege must appear in the state statute. Some examples of these privileges are: physician-patient, priest-penitent, attorney-client, and spousal privilege.
- Attorney Work Product. CPLR § 3101(c). This privilege encompasses the documents prepared by the attorney or someone working under the direction of the attorney (such as a paralegal, law clerk, or secretary) in anticipation of the litigation. It would include all research notes, interview notes taken in discussions with the client, and anything else that is the result of the attorney's thought process. The privilege belongs

to the attorney, and such material can only be discovered with the attorney's consent.

Example: *In preparation for trial, an attorney and his paralegal research the pertinent statutory and case law on the matter. While doing research, they jot down notes and thoughts with respect to the effect of this law on the merits of the client's case. These notes are considered the attorney's work product and are not subject to discovery.*

Qualified Privileges

The following items are generally privileged, but may be discovered, if so ordered by the court, in the interests of justice:

- Litigation material prepared by a nonattorney. In order to be privileged the material must have been prepared for the litigation in question.

Example: *After discussing a potential lawsuit with his attorney, a client has a bookkeeper prepare a list of disbursements that the client believes will be necessary for the lawsuit. This material prepared by the bookkeeper may be subject to discovery.*

- Witnesses' statements and the names of potential witnesses.

Example: *After a car accident an eyewitness calls the plaintiff's attorney and says that she saw the plaintiff run a red light, but she does not want to testify. The plaintiff must divulge the witness's name if asked for by the defendant.*

- Disclosure of insurance coverage.
- Accident reports when they were prepared in the regular course of business by governmental or private persons, except for reports prepared by the police as part of a criminal investigation if their disclosure would hamper the criminal investigation.

<u>Example</u>: Police officers have been investigating a man suspected of drug dealing. While following him, they witness a car accident in which he is involved and must make a report to the station. This report may not be discoverable if it may hamper the police investigation of the suspected drug dealer by alerting him of the investigation.

- Experts, but the substance of their potential testimony is discoverable, as are their names, to prepare the opposing attorney to cross-examine the expert at trial
- Films, photographs, videotapes, and audiotapes.

Privileges Subject to Special Limitations

The CPLR has specified the following special rules for specific types of lawsuits:

- *<u>Matrimonial Actions</u>*. Pretrial discovery on the merits is precluded.
- *<u>Shareholders' Derivative Actions</u>*. There must be a strong showing of essential need to discover internal corporate documents.
- *<u>Accounting Records</u>*. These are only discoverable if a right to access to the account has been established.
- *<u>Medical Malpractice Cases</u>*. The plaintiff cannot compel reports by the insurer or any report by the Board for Professional Medical Conduct.

Aside from the foregoing, all other material is subject to discovery.

Discovery Devices

In order to acquire the information necessary to prosecute or defend the lawsuit, the CPLR specifies five discovery devices that the litigants may employ:

Oral Depositions

An **oral deposition**, also known as an **examination before trial (EBT)**, permits a party to question an opposing party (or witness) under oath. The questions and answers are written down by a court reporter or stenographer, paid for by the party requesting the deposition and are then reduced to writing by the court reporter or stenographer.

To take an oral deposition the party requesting the deposition must send written notice to the party to be deposed at least 20 days before the deposition date (25 days if notice is sent by mail). The party to be deposed may serve a **cross-notice** to depose the original requesting party at least ten days before the deposition date (15 days if notice is sent by mail). If the person to be deposed, the deponent, is not a party to the action, the party requesting the deposition must serve the nonparty with a subpoena at least 20 days before the deposition date. A **subpoena** is an order by the court compelling the person named in the subpoena to attend. The oral deposition may be held in one of the following places:

1. To depose a resident party, the deposition may take place
   a. where the party resides
   b. at the party's office or
   c. where the trial is to be held.
2. To depose a nonresident party, the deposition may take place within New York at a mutually convenient location or by written questions that the party responds to in writing under oath. CPLR § 3109. The nonresident party may also be deposed by "open commission." (*see below*) CPLR § 3201.
3. To depose a corporate party, the deposition may take place at the place of business or the residence of the employee to be deposed. CPLR § 3110(1).
4. To depose public corporate entities, the deposition may take place in any county where the action is commenced. For the purpose of depositions, New York City is considered to be one county.

5. To depose a nonparty witness, the deposition may take place at the witness's residence, place of business if the witness resides or works in New York, or anywhere the witness may be subpoenaed if the witness is nonresident.

The deposition may be taken in the form of either written questions to which the deponent responds orally (sealed commission) or by open commission in which the questions and the responses are given orally. The deposition is taken under oath before a clerk of the court or a notary public (court reporters and stenographers are typically licensed as notary publics so that they may administer the oath). The defendant has the right to request a deposition first in his or her answer to the complaint, but if the defendant does not make a request for a deposition either side may commence the process. In order to take a deposition in a foreign country of a nonparty, the moving party must obtain a **letter rogatory**, court permission to take a foreign deposition.

A transcript of the deposition must be made and the transcript is required to be filed with the court, CPLR § 3116(b), but the filing is usually waived by stipulation of the parties. The deposition may be used at the trial against the party who was deposed, and can be used against nonparties in cross-examination. If a portion of the deposition is read in court, the entire deposition is deemed admissible.

<u>Example</u>: *On the witness stand a party to the action contradicts a statement he made under oath at his deposition. During cross-examination the party's statement may be challenged by the introduction of the deposition to impeach his credibility.*

Written Interrogatories

Written interrogatories are permitted pursuant to section 3130(34) of the CPLR and are a more economical method of discovery than depositions because court reporters are not needed and the attorneys representing each side do not have to attend. Furthermore, the party being deposed has the opportunity to think over his or her answers before responding, so the answers may be more accurate. However, there are certain limitations imposed in the area of written interrogatories.

- If the basis of the action is negligence, a court order is necessary to use written interrogatories.
- In multiple-theory actions, the parties may use both depositions and written interrogatories without court approval.
- Except for matrimonial actions, written interrogatories can be used without court approval.

If written interrogatories are used, the answer must be served within 20 days, and the answers must be made under oath.

<u>Example</u>: *In an antitrust action the attorney for the defendant decides to use the discovery device of written interrogatories in order to be cost efficient. The attorney does not believe that oral depositions will be more advantageous than written interrogatories with answers given under oath.*

Discovery and Inspection

Discovery and inspection is the term appearing under section 3312 of the CPLR for the examination of physical objects and documents under the control of the opposing side. Such evidence can be obtained from the party who controls it by sending a notice of request for the evidence 20 days in advance of the expected date of inspection. If the evidence is under the control of a nonparty, the party seeking discovery must file a notice with the court requesting the nonparty to provide the evidence subject to a subpoena.

If the party seeking discovery wishes to subject the object to scientific testing, the testing will be permitted only if it does not destroy the integrity of the object. Furthermore, discovery and inspection are usually not granted until after the Examination Before Trial has taken place.

<u>Example</u>: *A plaintiff has a document that supposedly proves her case. The defendant's position is that the document is forged. The document is supposed to be over 100 years old, and the defendant wishes to have it scientifically tested to determine its age. The testing will only be permitted if it will not destroy the integrity of the document.*

Physical Examination

A party may request the opposing side to submit to a physical or mental examination, but only if the party's physical or mental condition is part of the lawsuit, such as a claim for personal injury caused by the defendant. CPLR § 3121.The plaintiff's complaint asserting physical or mental injury is deemed to be a waiver of the plaintiff's privilege, and so all of the plaintiff's physical and mental records will be discoverable and the plaintiff must submit to physical and mental examination.

A defendant can only be asked to submit to a physical or mental examination if the defendant put his or her physical or mental condition in controversy. The physician-patient privilege is not waived if the defendant's condition is put in controversy by extra-judicial evidence such as a police accident report.

<u>Example</u>: *In his answer to the complaint for breach of contract, the defendant asserts that he has diminished capacity and therefore is legally incapable of entering into a valid contract. By his answer the defendant has placed his mental condition in controversy and is subject to having a mental examination at the plaintiff's request.*

<u>Example</u>: *After a car accident, the police report contained a statement by a witness that the defendant appeared to be limping badly before the accident took place. In this instance the defendant has not put his physical condition into controversy and is not required to submit to a physical examination.*

The cost of the examination is the responsibility of the party requesting it, and the party so examined is entitled to a copy of the examination results.

Notice to Admit and Demand for Address

In order to reduce litigable issues, the parties may decide that certain items be admitted. CPLR § 3118. The party who is asked to admit certain allegations must respond within 20 days of the demand under oath; a failure to reply to the demand or failing to deny it is deemed to be an **admission**.

Example: The plaintiff demands that the defendant admit that she was driving the car in question at the time of the accident. The defendant fails to deny the allegation so it is deemed admitted—the defendant is now conclusively determined to be the driver of the car at the time of the accident.

A party may demand the address of an opposing party, a co-party, the assignor of a claim or defense now asserted by the assignee, or the address of a corporate officer if the opposing party is a corporation.

Example: A tenant wants to sue her landlord but only has the address of the landlord's agent. The tenant sues the landlord and the agent, and once served the tenant can make a demand for the address of the landlord from the agent.

Discovery Motions

Parties are not always willing to submit voluntarily to the demands for discovery. Two types of motions are typically made by the parties during the discovery process, one on behalf of the person objecting to providing the information sought, and the other for the person requesting the discovery. However, the courts generally discourage discovery motions and prefer the parties to schedule a conference with the judge to resolve the matter outside of the courtroom.

Motion for a Protective Order

If a demand for discovery has been made to a party who believes that the matter is not discoverable, the party may make a motion to the court to limit or modify the demand. CPLR § 3103. These motions are made if the evidence sought is subject to a privilege, the evidence would be too burdensome to acquire, or the party seeking the material has already received adequate responses to the requests.

Example: *A shareholder is claiming breach of a fiduciary obligation by the corporate directors. During discovery he requests copies of all internal company memos written during the preceding five years. The directors move for a protective order claiming that the demand is overbroad, unduly burdensome, and represents a "fishing expedition" on the part of the shareholder in hopes of finding something upon which to base his claim.*

Motion to Compel

Conversely, the party seeking discovery can request the court to order a recalcitrant party to respond to its discovery demands. CPLR § 3124. If the court orders the party to respond to the discovery demand and the party still refuses to do so, the court can

- decide the issue against the non-delivering party
- prevent the nondelivering party from presenting evidence on the issue at trial
- strike the pleading containing the allegations subject to the evidence the party refuses to deliver
- hold the nondelivering party in contempt of court.

If the defendant refuses to respond to discovery demands because of a valid privilege assertion, the court will not issue sanctions. If the plaintiff, on the other hand, does so, the court may dismiss the complaint. Once the parties have completed the discovery process, the case is ready to go to trial.

Example: *A plaintiff alleges injuries and loss of income due to the defendant's negligence. She has been requested by the defendant to provide her engagement calendar for the period after the date of the accident. The plaintiff refuses, and the defendant asserts that the engagement calendar may contain proof of the plaintiff's physical activities after the alleged injury. The court agrees. If the plaintiff persists in refusing to provide the document, the court could dismiss the lawsuit or hold the plaintiff in contempt.*

Ethical Concerns

Many times the discovery process is used by the litigants to create delays and to harass the opposing party by making numerous and unwarranted requests for evidence that is basically irrelevant. For this reason courts tend to limit the discovery process with respect depositions and interrogatories, and additional interrogatories and depositions of parties are permitted only with leave of the court.

The purpose of discovery is to reduce the number of issues that must be tried, not to try the patience of the opposing side. Also, parties may attempt to thwart the discovery process by subterfuge in the answer and by refusing to admit certain simple facts simply to extend the discovery period in the hopes that the opposing side will try to settle just to be rid of the lawsuit.

Chapter Review

Discovery is the process of acquiring evidence to be used to litigate a matter. As a corollary, discovery can be used to streamline the litigation process by eliminating matters that either are not truly in controversy or are overwhelmingly in favor of one of the parties, making litigating the issue a waste of time. In this fashion the actual trial can be more efficient, both in respect to time and money.

Although the CPLR authorizes discovery of all matters material to the prosecution or defense of a lawsuit, certain matters are deemed privileged and therefore cannot be discovered. Such matters may only be discovered if the privilege is waived by the party holding the right, either expressly by specific grant or implicitly by putting a privileged matter in controversy.

To obtain nonprivileged information, the CPLR authorizes the following discovery devices:

- oral depositions
- written interrogatories
- discovery and inspection of physical objects and documents
- physical and mental examination
- admissions and demands for addresses.

If a party objects to the particular request, the party may seek a protective order from the court to avoid having to produce the requested information. Conversely, a party-seeking discovery can make a motion to the court to force a recalcitrant party to respond to a discovery request. If the party fails to adhere to a court order compelling discovery, the court may sanction the party by holding the party in contempt, dismissing the suit, or holding that issue against the non-responding side. Once discovery is completed, the parties may begin the trial.

Key Terms

Absolute privilege – evidentiary privileges and attorney work product

Admission (Notice to Admit) – party agreeing to the truth of a specific allegation

Attorney work product – all material prepared by an attorney or someone working under the attorney's direction prepared for potential litigation—it is not discoverable

Cross-notice – request for oral deposition made by a party who is already required to be deposed.

Demand for address – discovery device in which a party can obtain addresses of the opposing side

Discovery – pretrial period during which the parties find out what evidence the other side has

Evidence privilege – absolute privilege for certain relationships appearing in the state statute, such as the attorney-client privilege

Examination Before Trial (EBT) – New York's version of an oral deposition of the parties; must be completed prior to the discovery process

Letter rogatory – court order permitting depositions to be taken in a foreign country

Motion for a protective order – request to limit a discovery demand

Motion to compel – request to the court to force a recalcitrant party to respond to a discovery demand

Oral deposition – discovery device in which the party or witness is questioned under oath

Privilege – certain information that is not discoverable

Qualified privilege – certain information that may not be discoverable depending upon the interests of justice

Stipulation – agreement of the parties with respect to certain facts or issues

Subpoena – court order requiring a party to appear

Written interrogatories – discovery device in which parties and witnesses supply written answers to written questions

Edited Judicial Decisions

Mendelowitz v. Xerox Corp.
169 AD2d 300 (1991)

Plaintiff's decedent was employed by various agencies of the United States Government from October 1955 to August 1978 as a "xerographer," a job that allegedly required him to stand over copying machines virtually all of his working hours. In October 1988, he was diagnosed as having mesothelioma, a type of lung cancer, from which he died in February 1989, three months after he started this action against Xerox Corporation, the manufacturer of the copying machines he allegedly operated; after his death, his wife, as administratrix of his estate, was substituted as plaintiff. According to the complaint, decedent's cancer was caused by his inhalation of asbestos dust emanating from components, particularly a "heat fuser," incorporated into the copying machines he operated; the complaint also alleges, insofar as pertinent, that "[a]t all relevant times, defendant knew or should have known that asbestos was deleterious to health, carcinogenic and posed a health hazard to consumers, users, and others exposed to it."

Plaintiff served a notice of discovery pursuant to CPLR § 3120 demanding, in request number seven, "[c]opies of any books, articles or other medical information concerning the effects of asbestos exposure on human health and safety in the possession of the defendant prior to January 1, 1979," this date being shortly subsequent to decedent's retirement as a xerographer. While objecting to the request as "overbroad and unduly burdensome," defendant nevertheless volunteered that prior to January 1, 1979, it had maintained in its possession "standard reference material including, but not limited to, *American Industrial Hygiene Association Journal*, *Patty's Industrial Hygiene and Toxicology*, and *Industrial Environment: Its Evaluation and Control (OSHA)*"; it then offered, in the good-faith discussions required by *22 NYCRR 202.7*(a), to respond to a request for "specifically identified books, articles or other medical information" in its possession prior to January 1, 1979. Plaintiff's attorney countered with an offer to withdraw the request if defendant allowed him access to the library it maintains at its corporate headquarters in Rochester, New York, so that he might personally search there for any materials relating to the health effects of asbestos. This was rejected by defendant for unspecified reasons, and so the motion for a protective order was submitted. IAS vacated the request, characterizing it as "overly broad and vague."

Defendant asserts, albeit only through its attorney, that compliance with the request would require it "to comb through" and "literally review every book, periodical and reference material in its possession to ascertain whether any responsive materials existed"; such a "ferret[ing]" task, defendant further asserts, would require an enormous amount of employee time and "plainly constitute an undue burden." (Although not mentioned by defendant, perhaps note should also be taken of the unreasonable burden involved in making a copy of, say, a 1,000-page reference manual.) For his part, plaintiff's attorney stresses the importance of this information to the issues raised in the lawsuit; asserts "that every asbestos manufacturer has either by agreement or court order conducted a similar search"; further asserts that "thousands and thousands of documents, studies, articles and other literature" have been published on the health effects of asbestos; points out that he could not be expected to "divine" which of these were in defendant's possession prior to 1979; suggests that inasmuch as defendant is not in the business of mining or milling asbestos, "it is more likely than not" that the amount of literature it keeps on the subject is small; and argues, unrealistically, that defendant's offer to search for specifically identified books and articles "would require [it] to conduct essentially the same task * * * as required by the requests at issue," and thus would impose no less of a burden. In short, each party urges that the burden of specification should be on the other.

While it is not true, as it might once have been (*see, City of New York v. Friedberg & Assocs.*, 62 AD2d 407, 410; *Harnett v. Skandia Am. Reinsurance Corp.*, 60 AD2d 515; *Ganin v.* Janow, 86 AD2d 857, 858), that the designation of documents by the use of such phrases as "all," "all other," or "any and all" necessarily and automatically renders a request for documents pursuant to CPLR § 3120 improper (*see, Ensign Bank v. Gerald Modell, Inc.*, 163 AD2d 149, *citing Stevens v. Metropolitan Suburban Bus Auth.*, 117 AD2d 733, 734, in turn citing *Agricultural & Indus. Corp. v. Chemical Bank*, 94 AD2d 671, and *Palmieri v. Kilcourse*, 91 AD2d 657; *see also, Mestman v. Ariens Co.*, 135 AD2d 516, 517, *citing Scheinfeld v. Burlant*, 98 AD2d 603; *Matter of Bird*, 100 AD2d 784), it is true that the use of such phrases continues to be viewed as at least "some indication of a lack of the requisite specificity" (*Stevens v. Metropolitan Suburban Bus Auth., supra,* at *734*), and is still frowned upon (*see, Agricultural & Indus. Corp. v. Chemical Bank, supra*, 94 AD2d, at 672; *Dopf v. United Airlines*, 135 AD2d 453; *Zimmerman v. New York City Tr. Auth.*, 115 AD2d 738; *Nankof v. ARA Servs.*, 96 AD2d 493). Exceptions have been found "in certain limited circumstances" where "the use of these phrases may relate to specific subject matter" and thus does not impede a ready identification of the particular thing(s) to be produced (*Matter of Bird, supra* [all Federal tax returns prepared for a trust over a five-year period]; *see also, e.g., Palmieri v. Kilcourse, supra* [any and all medical records pertaining to the treatment of a particular patient by a particular doctor, which records were presumably maintained in a single file under the patient's name]; *Ensign Bank v. Gerald Modell, Inc., supra* [all items of collateral held under specifically identified pawn tickets]; *but see, e.g., Craig v. New York Tel. Co.*, 123 AD2d 580 [all investigation reports, internal memoranda and the like concerning the investigation into the causes of a fire "not otherwise privileged or protected," and copies of all rules and regulations concerning employee safety and protocol relating to fire safety for a two-year period, but not "all incident reports, memoranda and communications pertaining to the fire"]; *Scheinfeld v. Burlant, supra* [any and all records, correspondence, memoranda and/or notes pertaining to the transactions in issue]).But in the main, the cases have been scrupulous in their adherence to the requirement of the statute that the notice specify the things sought with "reasonable particularity," and it is simply not open to challenge that the burden of specification is on the requesting party (*see*, Siegel, *Practice Commentaries, McKinney's Consol. Laws of N.Y.*, Book 7B, CPLR § 3120:4, at 597 [reasonable particularity means a description of the thing to be produced sufficient "to enable the adverse party to identify it readily"]; 3A Weinstein-Korn-Miller, NY Civ. Prac., para. 3120.17 [unlike its Federal Rules of Civil Procedure rule 34 counterpart, CPLR § 3120 does not explicitly authorize a designation of the things to be produced by "category"]; Siegel, *N.Y. Prac.* § 362, at 528 [2d ed.] ["Asking for 'any and all' documents of a general description is usually unacceptable"]).

If one were to go to a law library and ask for a copy of McCormick, Evidence, cited in plaintiff's brief for the proposition that evidence of prior similar accidents is admissible for the purpose of showing that a manufacturer had notice of hazards associated with its product, the librarian no doubt would get the book. If, on the other hand, one were to ask the same librarian for any and all books, articles or other legal literature making reference to the admissibility of other accidents in a products case, the librarian probably would not be so accommodating. The problem has not so much to do with the volume as with the cataloguing of the literature on a particular subject. If we knew for a fact that defendant's Rochester library maintains a card catalogue categorizing "Asbestos, health effects of," or even just "Asbestos," as a separate subject, perhaps we would consider directing defendant to supply a list of all of the books so categorized; we might even indulge in the assumption, absent proof to the contrary, that all such books published before January 1, 1979, were acquired by defendant before decedent's retirement. But the fact is that we do not know whether defendant maintains such a catalogue; indeed, we do not even know whether anyone anywhere else has undertaken to catalogue the literature on the health effects of asbestos.

Most fields of knowledge have recognized authorities. A lawyer concerned with a matter of New York practice would surely be aware of, and would probably consult, the Practice Commentaries in McKinney's Consolidated Laws of New York's Civil Practice Law and Rules, New York Civil Practice by Weinstein-Korn-Miller, and New York Practice by David D. Siegel. An on-point citation from any one of these works is usually enough to put a lawyer on notice, as it were, as to whether, and how far, that point has been accepted in authoritative legal circles. We know for a fact, by way of judicial notice, that asbestos dust is harmful to health; such is an accepted proposition in authoritative circles. What we do not know is when this proposition was first advanced, how much resistance it met, when it became settled and noncontroversial, and the identity of the experts who participated in creating and then reporting the consensus. But surely plaintiff's lawyer knows this, just as he knows of McKinney's Practice Commentaries, Weinstein-Korn-Miller, and Siegel, and we see no reason why he should not be content to begin his inquiry into defendant's knowledge concerning the hazards of asbestos by simply inquiring of it whether the works of any of the leading, consensus-creating and consensus-reporting authorities were contained in its library prior to 1979.Other avenues of inquiry suggest themselves as well and might be successfully pursued, such as service of a notice pursuant to CPLR § 3120(a)(1)(ii) permitting inspection of defendant's Rochester library for a reasonable period under appropriate safeguards, and service of a notice pursuant to CPLR § 3107 to take the deposition of defendant's Rochester librarian (*Rios v. Donovan*, 21 AD2d 409).

A second request in plaintiff's notice of discovery, number nine, sought "Lists of any claims and lawsuits filed against the defendant by any * * * person[s] [other than its own employees] in which personal injuries or death as a result of asbestos exposure to defendant's copying equipment [was claimed], setting forth the name and address of each claimant [and] if a lawsuit the name of the Court, court number and status of the case." In its motion for a protective order, defendant argued that this request is improper in that it is not limited to claims and lawsuits involving the particular models of copiers allegedly operated by decedent, or at least models shown to be substantially similar (*citing, inter alia, D'Alessio v. Nabisco, Inc.*, 123 AD2d 816; *Zimmerman v. New York City Tr. Auth.*, 115 AD2d 738; *Petty v. Riverbay Corp.*, 92 AD2d 525; *Ruggles v. White Metal Rolling & Stamping Corp.*, 86 AD2d 847; *Matos v. City of New York*, 78 AD2d 834; *Bertocci v. Fiat Motors*, 76 AD2d 779; *Savitsky v. General Motors Corp.*, 40 AD2d 1025). IAS agreed, stating that "[p]laintiff has not shown that other copier models are substantially similar to those utilized by decedent, or shown how information pertaining to other copiers would be relevant to this matter," and pruned the request to include only "copier models utilized by decedent."

Although defendant does not make a point of it, we think it pertinent that the request is more in the nature of an interrogatory than a demand for discovery. Plaintiff is not asking that any particular documents or other tangible things be produced; rather, as her lawyer made clear in opposing the protective order, what she seeks is a list of any claims or lawsuits brought against defendant for injury or death allegedly caused "by inhalation of asbestos dust from copying equipment manufactured, sold and distributed by Xerox from the period of time commencing with its earliest made copying equipment to date." While the reference in the notice to "claims" is indeed vague, and should therefore be disregarded, it is eminently reasonable to assume that if in fact any asbestos-related lawsuits have been brought against defendant, it maintains easily accessible files concerning such; and if, for some reason, defendant should not be able to supply a list of such lawsuits that is exhaustive, it need only say so in a sworn statement.

We see absolutely no merit to defendant's argument that the list plaintiff seeks should be limited to lawsuits involving the same models of copiers allegedly operated by decedent, and completely agree with plaintiff that what makes these other lawsuits material and necessary and substantially similar to her own is the common allegation of exposure to a copying machine, whatever the model, that was manufactured by defendant with an asbestos-containing component. With respect, we think it disingenuous of defendant to suggest in the context of disclosure—without taking issue with plaintiff's assertion that there is no known safe level of exposure to asbestos dust, and without coming in with proof that any of its asbestos-containing models of copiers was specifically designed to abate the risk of asbestos exposure—that asbestos housed in other models presented less of a threat to health than the allegedly asbestos-containing models used by decedent. The weight to be given evidence of other injuries or deaths on the issues of notice and causation, and indeed the very admissibility of such evidence for whatever purpose plaintiff may want it introduced, are not of concern in the context of disclosure. At this juncture, the concern is with the usefulness and reasonableness of the list plaintiff asks defendant to compile in aiding preparation for trial (*Allen v. Crowell-Collier Publ. Co.*, 21 NY2d 403, 406–407); with that in mind, we think the list should be supplied if only because it could be useful in facilitating communication among persons who have good reason to think of themselves as similarly situated.

A third request in plaintiff's notice of discovery, number eight, sought "A list of all health claims made by any workers of the defendant alleging adverse health effects as a result of asbestos exposure." Defendant argued successfully before IAS that this request is improper in that it is not limited to copying machines "and would even encompass claims made by workers alleging exposure to asbestos contained in, for example, building insulation." We agree—evidence of health claims made by defendant's employees that are not somehow connected with the manufacture of defendant's copying machines would not be useful in prosecuting the claim made in this lawsuit. However, rather than vacate the request in its entirety, as IAS did, we think it better to prune it to include only "a list of all health claims made by any workers of the defendant alleging adverse health effects as a result of exposure to asbestos used in the manufacture of copying machines." We again emphasize that the disclosure of evidence, and its admissibility at trial, are completely separate matters.

Accordingly, the order of the Supreme Court, Bronx County (Hansel L. McGee, J.), entered March 23, 1990, which granted defendant's motion for a protective order to the extent of vacating plaintiff's requests number seven and eight and partially vacating so much of request number nine as sought a list of claims and lawsuits filed against defendant alleging exposure to asbestos as a result of using models of defendant's copying machines other than the models allegedly used by decedent, should be modified, on the law, the facts and in the exercise of discretion, to partially reinstate request number eight so as to limit it to a list of health claims made by defendant's employees alleging exposure to asbestos used in the manufacture of copying machines, and to reinstate request number nine to the extent it seeks a list of lawsuits, and otherwise affirmed, without costs.

Niesig v. Team I
76 NY2d 363 (1990)

Plaintiff in this personal injury litigation, wishing to have his counsel privately interview a corporate defendant's employees who witnessed the accident, puts before us a question that has generated wide interest: are the employees of a corporate party also considered "parties" under Disciplinary Rule 7-104(A)(1) of the Code of Professional Responsibility, which prohibits a lawyer from communicating directly with a "party" known to have counsel in the matter? The trial court and the Appellate Division both answered that an employee of a counseled corporate party in litigation is by definition also a "party" within the rule, and prohibited the interviews. For reasons of policy, we disagree.

As alleged in the complaint, plaintiff was injured when he fell from scaffolding at a building construction site. At the time of the accident he was employed by DeTrae Enterprises, Inc.; defendant J.M. Frederick was the general contractor, and defendant Team I the property owner. Plaintiff thereafter commenced a damages action against defendants, asserting two causes of action centering on Labor Law § 240, and defendants brought a third-party action against DeTrae.

Plaintiff moved for permission to have his counsel conduct *ex parte* interviews of all DeTrae employees who were on the site at the time of the accident, arguing that these witnesses to the event were neither managerial nor controlling employees and could not therefore be considered "personal synonyms for DeTrae." DeTrae opposed the application, asserting that the disciplinary rule barred unapproved contact by plaintiff's lawyer with any of its employees. Supreme Court denied plaintiff's request, and the Appellate Division modified by limiting the ban to DeTrae's current employees.

The Appellate Division concluded, for theoretical as well as practical reasons, that current employees of a corporate defendant in litigation "are presumptively within the scope of the representation afforded by the attorneys who appeared [in the litigation] on behalf of that corporation." (149 AD2d 94, 95.) Citing *Upjohn Co. v. United States* (449 U.S. 383), the court held that DeTrae's attorneys have an attorney-client relationship with every DeTrae employee connected with the subject of the litigation, and that the prohibition is necessitated by the practical difficulties of distinguishing between a corporation's control group and its other employees. The court further noted that the information sought from employee witnesses could instead be obtained through their depositions.

In the main we disagree with the Appellate Division's conclusions. However, because we agree with the holding that DR 7-104(A)(1) applies only to current employees, not to former employees, we modify rather than reverse its order, and grant plaintiff's motion to allow the interviews.

We begin our analysis by noting that what is at issue is a disciplinary rule, not a statute. In interpreting statutes, which are the enactments of a coequal branch of government and an expression of the public policy of this State, we are of course bound to implement the will of the Legislature; statutes are to be applied as they are written or interpreted to effectuate the legislative intention. The disciplinary rules have a different provenance and purpose. Approved by the New York State Bar Association and then enacted by the Appellate Divisions, the Code of Professional Responsibility is essentially the legal profession's document of self-governance, embodying principles of ethical conduct for attorneys as well as rules for professional discipline (*see*, *Code of Professional Responsibility, Preliminary Statement*, McKinney's Consol. Law of N.Y., Book 29, at 355). While unquestionably important, and respected by the courts, the code does not have the force of law (*see*, *Matter of Weinstock*, 40 NY2d 1, 6).

That distinction is particularly significant when a disciplinary rule is invoked in litigation, which in addition to matters of professional conduct by attorneys, implicates the interests of non-lawyers (*see, S & S Hotel Ventures Ltd. Partnership v 777 S. H. Corp.*, 69 NY2d 437, 443). In such instances, we are not constrained to read the rules literally or effectuate the intent of the drafters, but look to the rules as guidelines to be applied with due regard for the broad range of interests at stake. "When we agree that the Code applies in an equitable manner to a matter before us, we should not hesitate to enforce it with vigor. When we find an area of uncertainty, however, we must use our judicial process to make our own decision in the interests of justice to all concerned." (*Id.* [quoting *Foley & Co. v. Vanderbilt*, 523 F2d 1357, 1360 (2d Cir., Gurfein, J., concurring)].)

DR 7-104(A)(1), which can be traced to the American Bar Association Canons of 1908, fundamentally embodies principles of fairness." The general thrust of the rule is to prevent situations in which a represented party may be taken advantage of by adverse counsel; the presence of the party's attorney theoretically neutralizes the contact." (*Wright v. Group Health Hosp.*, 103 Wash. 2d 192, 197, 691 P.2d 564, 567.) By preventing lawyers from deliberately dodging adversary counsel to reach—and exploit—the client alone, DR 7-104(A)(1) safeguards against clients making improvident settlements, ill-advised disclosures and unwarranted concessions (*see*, 1 Hazard & Hodes, *Lawyering*, at 434–435 [1989 Supp.]; Wolfram, *Modern Legal Ethics* § 11.6, at 613 [Practitioner's ed. 1986]; Leubsdorf, *Communicating with Another Lawyer's Client: The Lawyer's Veto and the Client's Interests*, 127 U. Pa. L. Rev. 683, 686 [1979]).

There is little problem applying DR 7-104(A)(1) to individuals in civil cases. In that context, the meaning of "party" is ordinarily plain enough: it refers to the individuals, not to their agents and employees (*see*, Gillers & Dorsen, *Regulation of Lawyers: Problems of Law and Ethics*, at 433 [2d ed. 1989]). The question, however, becomes more difficult when the parties are corporations—as evidenced by a wealth of commentary, and controversy, on the issue (citations omitted).

The difficulty is not in whether DR 7-104(A)(1) applies to corporations. It unquestionably covers corporate parties, who are as much served by the rule's fundamental principles of fairness as individual parties. But the rule does not define "party," and its reach in this context is unclear. In litigation only the entity, not its employee, is the actual named party; on the other hand, corporations act solely through natural persons, and unless some employees are also considered parties, corporations are effectively read out of the rule. The issue therefore distills to which corporate employees should be deemed parties for purposes of DR 7-104(A)(1), and that choice is one of policy. The broader the definition of "party" in the interests of fairness to the corporation, the greater the cost in terms of foreclosing vital informal access to facts.

The many courts, bar associations and commentators that have balanced the competing considerations have evolved various tests, each claiming some adherents, each with some imperfection (*see generally, Annotation, Right of Attorney to Conduct Ex Parte Interviews with Corporate Party's Nonmanagement Employees*, 50 ALR4th 652 [1986] [collecting cases]). At one extreme is the blanket rule adopted by the Appellate Division and urged by defendants, and at the other is the "control group" test—both of which we reject. The first is too broad and the second too narrow.

Defendants' principal argument for the blanket rule—correlating the corporate "party" and all of its employees—rests on *Upjohn v. United States* (449 U.S. 383, *supra*). As the Supreme Court recognized, a corporation's attorney-client privilege includes communications with low- and mid-level employees; defendants argue that the existence of an attorney-client privilege also signifies an attorney-client relationship for purposes of DR 7-104(A)(1).

Upjohn, however, addresses an entirely different subject, with policy objectives that have little relation to the question whether a corporate employee should be considered a "party" for purposes of the disciplinary rule. First, the privilege applies only to confidential communications with counsel (*see*, CPLR § 4503), it does not immunize the underlying factual information—which is in issue here—from disclosure to an adversary (*see also, Upjohn v. United States*, 449 U.S., at 395–396, *supra*). Second, the attorney-client privilege serves the societal objective of encouraging open communication between client and counsel (*see*, *Rossi v. Blue Cross & Blue Shield*, 73 NY2d 588, 592), a benefit not present in denying informal access to factual information. Thus, a corporate employee who may be a "client" for purposes of the attorney-client privilege is not necessarily a "party" for purposes of DR 7-104(A)(1).

The single indisputable advantage of a blanket preclusion—as with every absolute rule—is that it is clear. No lawyer need ever risk disqualification or discipline because of uncertainty as to which employees are covered by the rule and which not. The problem, however, is that a ban of this nature exacts a high price in terms of other values, and is unnecessary to achieve the objectives of DR 7-104(A)(1).

Most significantly, the Appellate Division's blanket rule closes off avenues of informal discovery of information that may serve both the litigants and the entire justice system by uncovering relevant facts, thus promoting the expeditious resolution of disputes. Foreclosing all direct, informal interviews of employees of the corporate party unnecessarily sacrifices the long-recognized potential value of such sessions." A lawyer talks to a witness to ascertain what, if any, information the witness may have relevant to his theory of the case, and to explore the witness' knowledge, memory and opinion—frequently in light of information counsel may have developed from other sources. This is part of an attorney's so-called work product." (*International Business Machs. Corp. v. Edelstein*, 526 F2d 37, 41 [*citing Hickman v. Taylor*, 329 U.S. 495].) Costly formal depositions that may deter litigants with limited resources, or even somewhat less formal and costly interviews attended by adversary counsel, are no substitute for such off-the-record private efforts to learn and assemble, rather than perpetuate, information.

Nor, in our view, is it necessary to shield all employees from informal interviews in order to safeguard the corporation's interest. Informal encounters between a lawyer and an employee-witness are not—as a blanket ban assumes—invariably calculated to elicit unwitting admissions; they serve long-recognized values in the litigation process. Moreover, the corporate party has significant protection at hand. It has possession of its own information and unique access to its documents and employees; the corporation's lawyer thus has the earliest and best opportunity to gather the facts, to elicit information from employees, and to counsel and prepare them so that they will not make the feared improvident disclosures that engendered the rule.

We fully recognize that, as the Appellate Division observed, every rule short of the absolute poses practical difficulties as to where to draw the line, and leaves some uncertainty as to which employees fall on either side of it. Nonetheless, we conclude that the values served by permitting access to relevant information require that an effort be made to strike a balance, and that uncertainty can be minimized if not eliminated by a clear test that will become even clearer in practice.

We are not persuaded, however, that the "control group" test—defining "party" to include only the most senior management exercising substantial control over the corporation—achieves that goal. Unquestionably, that narrow (though still uncertain) definition of corporate "party" better serves the policy of promoting open access to relevant information. However, that test gives insufficient regard to the principles motivating DR 7-104(A)(1), and wholly overlooks the fact that corporate employees other than senior management also can bind the corporation. The "control group" test all but "nullifies the benefits of the disciplinary rule to corporations." (*Comment, Ex Parte Communications with Corporate Parties: The Scope of the Limitations on Attorney Communications with One of Adverse Interest, 82 Nw. U. L. Rev. 1274, 1288 [1988]; see also, Morrison v. Brandeis Univ.*, 125 FRD 14, 16–17 [D Mass]; *Massa v. Eaton Corp.*, 109 FRD 312, 313–314 [W.D. Mich.].) Given the practical and theoretical problems posed by the "control group" test, it is hardly surprising that few courts or bar associations have ever embraced it.

By the same token, we find unsatisfactory several of the proposed intermediate tests, because they give too little guidance, or otherwise seem unworkable. In this category are the case-by-case balancing test (*see, B. H. v. Johnson,* 128 FRD 659 [ND Ill]; *Morrison v. Brandeis Univ., supra),* and a test that defines "party" to mean corporate employees only when they are interviewed about matters within the scope of their employment (Committee on Professional Ethics, Assn. of Bar of City of N.Y., Opn. No. 80-46 [1980]; Committee on Professional Ethics, Massachusetts Bar Assn., Formal Opn. No. 82-7 [1982]). The latter approach is based on rule 801(d)(2)(D) of the Federal Rules of Evidence, a hearsay exception for statements concerning matters within the scope of employment, which is different from the New York State rule (*see, Loschiavo v. Port Auth.*, 58 NY2d 1040; *Kelly v. Diesel Constr. Div.*, 35 NY2d 1).

The test that best balances the competing interests, and incorporates the most desirable elements of the other approaches, is one that defines "party" to include corporate employees whose acts or omissions in the matter under inquiry are binding on the corporation (in effect, the corporation's "alter egos") or imputed to the corporation for purposes of its liability, or employees implementing the advice of counsel. All other employees may be interviewed informally.

Unlike a blanket ban or a "control group" test, this solution is specifically targeted at the problem addressed by DR 7-104(A)(1). The potential unfair advantage of extracting concessions and admissions from those who will bind the corporation is negated when employees with "speaking authority" for the corporation, and employees who are so closely identified with the interests of the corporate party as to be indistinguishable from it, are deemed "parties" for purposes of DR 7-104(A)(1).Concern for the protection of the attorney-client privilege prompts us also to include in the definition of "party" the corporate employees responsible for actually effectuating the advice of counsel in the matter (*see*, *Polycast Technology Corp. v. Uniroyal, Inc.*, 129 FRD 621, 625, 628, 629 [SD NY]; 1 Hazard & Hodes, op. cit., at 436–437).

In practical application, the test we adopt thus would prohibit direct communication by adversary counsel "with those officials, but only those, who have the legal power to bind the corporation in the matter or who are responsible for implementing the advice of the corporation's lawyer, or any member of the organization whose own interests are directly at stake in a representation." (Wolfram, op. cit., § 11.6, at 613.) This test would permit direct access to all other employees, and specifically—as in the present case—it would clearly permit direct access to employees who were merely witnesses to an event for which the corporate employer is sued.

Apart from striking the correct balance, this test should also become relatively clear in application. It is rooted in developed concepts of the law of evidence and the law of agency, thereby minimizing the uncertainty facing lawyers about to embark on employee interviews. A similar test, moreover, is the one overwhelmingly adopted by courts and bar associations throughout the country, whose long practical experience persuades us that—in day-to-day operation—it is workable.

Finally, we note the particular contribution made by the various *amici curiae* in this case; by highlighting the diverse contexts in which the question may arise, their submissions have enlarged our comprehension of the broad potential impact of the issue presented. In so doing, however, they have also alerted us to the wisdom of flagging what is in any event implicit in our decisions—that they are limited by the facts before us and the questions put to us. Today's decision resolves the present controversy by allowing *ex parte* interviews with nonmanagerial witnesses employed by a corporate defendant; even in that limited context, we recognize that there are undoubtedly questions not raised by the parties that will yet have to be answered. Defendants' assertions that *ex parte* interviews should not be permitted because of the dangers of overreaching, moreover, impel us to add the cautionary note that, while we have not been called upon to consider questions relating to the actual conduct of such interviews, it is of course assumed that attorneys would make their identity and interest known to interviewees and comport themselves ethically.

Accordingly, the order of the Appellate Division should be modified, without costs, by reversing so much of the Appellate Division order as denied plaintiff's motion to permit *ex parte* interviews of current DeTrae employees and, as so modified, the Appellate Division order should be affirmed and the certified question answered in the negative.

Exercises

1. Many form books provide sample questions for written interrogatories. Indicate three such books.

2. Everyone acknowledges that privileges exist. Why should certain information be privileged? Explain.

3. What is your opinion of the sanctions a court may impose on a party who refuses to comply with discovery demands? Explain.

4. Discuss in detail your opinion of the discovery process.

5. Why should an attorney's work product be an absolute privilege? Explain.

Exhibit

SUBPOENA DUCES TECUM

INDEX NUMBER

THE PEOPLE OF THE STATE OF NEW YORK TO, ________

GREETINGS:

WE COMMAND YOU, that all business and excuses being laid aside you appear and attend before one of the justices of our Court at a Term, Part 1, thereof, to be held in and for the County of Kings at the courthouse in the City of New York __________ on the day of, 2000, at ________ o'clock in the afternoon, to testify and give evidence in a certain action now pending undetermined in said court between, plaintiff, and, defendant, on the part of plaintiff and that you bring with you and produce at that time and place aforesaid, the following {set forth papers to be produced}

WITNESS, Hon. ________________, one of the Justices of our said Court, at the Kings County Court House in Brooklyn, New York, on the day of 2000.

____

{Print Name}
Clerk

{Seal of Court}

____

Attorney for Plaintiff
Address:

Chapter Six

TRIAL

Introduction

This chapter is concerned exclusively with procedures involved in a civil trial; it is not intended to discuss evidentiary rules or strategies for conducting a trial. These topics are more appropriately left to texts on those specific topics.

The trial process commences at the termination of the discovery process (*see* Chapter Five). In order to begin the trial, the plaintiff must file a **notice of issue** with the clerk of the court to have the case placed on the court calendar. A note of issue may be filed at any time after 40 days following the service of the summons on the defendant. Along with the note of issue, the plaintiff may make a **demand for a jury trial**; the other party to the lawsuit may file a jury demand independently if not done so by the plaintiff.

Example: *In her note of issue, the plaintiff does not request a jury trial because she would prefer to have her case decided by the judge. When the defendant receives notice of the note of issue, he may make his own demand for a jury trial. Each party has the right to a trial by jury if the issues in the case so warrant, and no party may preclude a jury trial if the other side desires one.*

Cases are placed on the court calendar according to the following preferences:

1. cases brought by the state of New York, a state official, or a political subdivision
2. cases that are given a specific preference by statute, such as cases seeking injunctions

3. cases in which the court believes a preference should be granted in the interests of justice
4. cases in which a party is 70 years of age or older
5. medical or dental malpractice cases (In this instance, the plaintiff must file for a preference within 60 days after the issue is joined. These cases also require precalendar conferences [CPLR § 3406(a)].)
6. personal injury cases in which the plaintiff is terminally ill due to the alleged negligence of the defendant.

The role of the paralegal with respect to the actual trial preparation is multi-faceted. The paralegal aids the attorney in the **pretrial conference** (a meeting between the parties and the judge who will preside over the case in order to limit the triable issues); prepares an evidence log to be used by the attorney during the actual litigation; helps select a shadow jury if the attorney believes such a practice would be helpful; assists in preparing the witnesses prior to trial; and keeps track of all papers filed with the court.

<u>Example</u>: *In preparing for the trial, the paralegal places all of the evidence in an* ***evidence log*** *in the order the attorney has decided the evidence will be presented at trial. The paralegal helps the attorney to prepare the witnesses by asking them the types of questions they will be asked in the witness stand and explaining the trial procedure to the witnesses. The paralegal also maintains a log of all documents filed in the case.*

In addition to the foregoing, a paralegal may be called upon to research case and statutory law relating to the appropriateness of the evidence the attorney plans to present at trial or with respect to potential objections to evidence and testimony the opposing side will present.

Trial by Jury

Any party to a lawsuit may make a demand for a jury trial as of right for the following types of lawsuits:

- cases in which the only relief requested is money judgment
- cases involving ejectment, claims for abatement and recovery of damages for nuisance, actions to recover chattels, claims involving waste, and claims relating to real estate
- cases in which a jury trial has been provided for by contract or statute.

A party to a lawsuit may waive his or her right to a jury determination by any of the following means:

- agreeing to a waiver of a jury trial in a contract with the opposing party
- failing to make a demand for a jury trial
- joining both legal and equitable claims in the same suit
- making a waiver of a jury trial in open court.

Example: *A plaintiff brings suit for ejectment against a trespasser to his property. The plaintiff does not want a jury trial and so made no jury demand in his note of issue. The defendant would have preferred a jury trial, but neglected to make a jury demand. In this instance, this case will be tried by the bench.*

For a civil case in a New York state court the jury need only be composed of six members, and the court may provide for one or two alternate jurors in case a jury member must be dismissed during the course of the trial. For a verdict, five of the six members must agree.

The jury selection process, known as ***voir dire*** (a French phrase meaning "to speak the truth"), is conducted in open court in which each side is afforded the opportunity to question potential jury members regarding potential conflicts of interest, bias or prejudice with respect to the case or the parties. Each side may dismiss as many potential jurors as they want for just cause, and may dismiss a specific number of potential jurors simply because they do not want that particular person on the jury with what is known as a **peremptory challenge**.

Example: *The jury for a potential case is composed of six jurors and one alternate. Midway through the trial the spouse of one of the jurors becomes gravely ill and the juror requests to be relieved to take care of the spouse. If the court agrees, the juror will be excused and the alternate juror, who is required to attend the entire trial, will replace the dismissed juror so that the trial may go on.*

At the conclusion of the trial the judge is required to instruct the jury with respect to the law to be applied to the facts they are mandated to determine. All parties to the lawsuit may request the court to issue specific instructions to the jury, and these jury instruction requests must be made to the judge prior to the court's summation. The judge will rule on these instruction requests prior to the summation. If any party objects to a specific jury instruction, the judge must rule on the objection before the jury retires for deliberation.

Example: *In a case involving interpretation of a contract covered by Article II of the Uniform Commercial Code, the plaintiff submits a request for a specific jury instruction concerning the legal definition of a "merchant." The judge agrees to the request before summing up the case for the jury. Opposing counsel objects to the specific instruction read and makes the objection before the jury retires. The objection may provide the legal basis for an appeal* (see *Chapter Seven).*

Jury Verdicts

At the conclusion of the case, the jury retires to reach a decision on the merits, known as a **verdict**. When at least five of the six jurors agree, the jury will notify the court and return to the courtroom to declare its verdict to the court. There are three types of verdicts that the jury can enter.

1. In a **general verdict** the jury simply states the ultimate conclusion, finding for either the plaintiff or defendant
2. In a **special verdict** the jury indicates the specific findings of fact upon which it based its decision. If the ultimate decision

reached by the jury is not substantiated by the findings of fact, the judge may order the jury to retire to reconsider the case.

3. In a **general verdict accompanied by answers to interrogatories** the jury is asked to answer specific questions that have been submitted to them regarding the specific evidence presented. If the jury's answers are inconsistent, the losing party may move the court
   a. for a new trial
   b. to direct the jury to reconsider or
   c. to overturn the jury's verdict.

These motions are called **posttrial motions** and will be discussed below.

In all tort actions, the jury is required to specify the amount of the special and general damages separately. CPLR § 4111(d), (f).

The losing side may attack the jury's verdict if

- the ultimate decision is contrary to the weight of the evidence, or
- as a matter of law, the verdict must be set aside because it is contrary to law.

Example: *In a case involving the value of a government license, the defendant presents evidence that includes his own testimony, the testimony of a government official of the agency issuing the license, and an independent business person who is in the business of using such licenses. All three witnesses agree on a value of $50,000. For the plaintiff, the plaintiff alone testifies to the value, indicating his personal belief that the value of the license is worth "millions." The jury finds for the plaintiff. The defendant may ask the court to set aside the verdict because the verdict went against the weight of the evidence presented at trial.*

Trial by Court

If there is no right to a jury trial, or the right has been waived, the facts in dispute are determined by the presiding judge in what is known as a **bench trial**. On its own initiative or in response to a motion made by one of the parties, the court may submit the matter to an **advisory jury** or **referee** who will submit its findings to the judge, but the judge always makes the final decision. The presiding judge merely listens to the advice of these persons.

<u>Example</u>: *In a complicated tax matter, the judge refers the issue of the value of the alleged liability to a referee who is experienced in tax matters. When the referee files her report, the judge remains free to make his own decision regardless of the referee's findings.*

The parties to the lawsuit may agree by stipulation that a referee can determine the issues, but may only so stipulate with the leave of the court in the following matters:

- matrimonial actions
- actions to dissolve a corporation
- actions in which the defendant is legally an infant.

In these situations, the decision of the referee is equivalent to the decision of the court.

<u>Example</u>: *In a breach of contract proceeding the parties want to have the amount of damages to be determined by a referee. They make a request to the court to have the referee decide these issues, and the judge agrees. The decision of the referee has the weight of a judicial decision in this instance.*

Trial Motions

During the actual trial proceedings, either party may make the following motions to the court:

Motion for Summary Judgment

At the conclusion of either the plaintiff's or the defendant's presentation, either side may move for a summary judgment. A motion for summary judgment is made when the moving party believes that there are no facts or laws in dispute, only the necessity to apply the law to the undisputed facts. If there are any facts in dispute, the court cannot grant the motion for summary judgment.

<u>Example</u>: *At the conclusion of the plaintiff's case in chief the plaintiff moves for a summary judgment. The lawsuit involves an accident and the plaintiff's evidence indicates that the defendant was exceeding the speed limit at the time the accident occurred. The defendant, however, asserts that she will prove in her case in chief that the plaintiff was responsible for the accident by jumping out into the road between parked cars and against the light. Because there are still facts in dispute, the motion will not be granted.*

Motion for a Directed Verdict

At the conclusion of either the plaintiff's or the defendant's case in chief, either side may make a **motion for a directed verdict**. This motion asks the judge to order the jury to find for the moving party based on the law and the facts presented. This motion basically precludes the jury from making deliberations, although the verdict is deemed to be the jury's. Motions for directed verdicts, because they are contrary to the concept of trial by jury, are often requested but rarely granted.

<u>Example</u>: *At the conclusion of the presentation of both sides' evidence, both the plaintiff and the defendant move for directed verdicts. The judge is unwilling to preclude the jury from making its own decision, and so denies the motions.*

Posttrial Motions

After the verdict has been reached, any party who disagrees, in whole or in part, with the verdict may make one of the following posttrial motions:

Motion for a New Trial

This motion is rarely granted, but it might be allowed in situations in which a party can show jury prejudice, jury tampering, or a decision that is contrary to the evidence presented.

Example: *After a verdict is rendered in favor of the defendant, the plaintiff discovers that one of the jury members is a relative of the defendant. This was not disclosed during the jury selection. This partiality on the part of a juror could constitute grounds for a motion for a new trial.*

Motion to Reconsider

With this motion, the party is requesting the court to order the jury to retire again to reconsider the verdict because the ultimate decision is not established by the findings of fact the jury has indicated.

Motion for a Judgment Notwithstanding the Verdict (Motion for a Judgment Non Obstante Veredicto *[JNOV])*

In this instance, rather than asking the court to have the jury reconsider the matter, the party requests the judge to render a verdict opposite to the jury's findings because the verdict is not substantiated by the evidence or is in conflict with the law. Motions for JNOV are almost always raised by the losing side but are not usually granted. The judge would rather have the verdict appealed (*see* Chapter Seven).

Example: *In the earlier example concerning the value of the government license, rather than moving to have the jury reconsider the matter the defendant may make a motion for a JNOV directly for the judge's action.*

Effects of the Decision

Once the jury has rendered its verdict and the court has entered its judgment, the issues are deemed conclusively determined with respect to the parties, absent an appeal. The effect of this is to preclude the parties from raising these issues again in another lawsuit against the same party according to the following doctrines:

Res Judicata

Res judicata mandates that because the claims of the parties have already been determined they may not be raised again. It is sometimes referred to as a "claims preclusion." The concept of res judicata only applies in instances in which there has been a judgment on the merits, not one based on a default judgment. The theory of res judicata does not apply to bankruptcy proceedings or arbital awards (*see* Chapter Eight).

If the matter is deemed res judicata, it is an affirmative defense of either party should the claim be attempted again in another forum or at a later date in the same forum.

Example: Pursuant to the long-arm statute a New York resident sues a Pennsylvania defendant for injuries resulting from a car accident in the state court of New York. There is a full trial, and the jury finds for the defendant. Neither side notes an appeal. Three months later the plaintiff brings a lawsuit against the defendant in the Pennsylvania court based on the same accident. The defendant may move to dismiss the suit based on the doctrine of res judicata.

Collateral Estoppel

The concept of **collateral estoppel** is similar to that of res judicata, but it concerns the issues decided in the first lawsuit, not necessarily the parties or the claim. It is therefore sometimes referred to as "issue preclusion." In order for a party to assert a claim of collateral estoppel, the following factors must be present:

- The issue in the present case is identical to the earlier decision.
- The issue must have been decided in order to reach the ultimate conclusion rendered in the earlier decision.
- The litigant must have had a full and fair opportunity to litigate the issue in the earlier proceeding.

The doctrine of collateral estoppel applies to all forms of litigation, but does not bar the same issue being tried both civilly and criminally, because the civil action concerns injury to a private person whereas the criminal proceeding involves injury to the state representing society as a whole.

<u>Example</u>: *As the result of a plane crash, a class action is instituted against the airline for negligence. The representative of the estate of one of the passengers is notified of the action, but opts out of the class. The jury finds that the airline was not negligent. After the decision is reached, the estate representative institutes an individual suit against the airline for negligence. The airline can assert that the issue on negligence is collaterally estopped from being litigated, based on the earlier trial.*

Settlement

At any time during the litigation proceedings, up to and including the time before a verdict has been rendered, the parties to the lawsuit may reach an agreement between and among themselves with respect to liability. This agreement is known as a **settlement** and is usually encouraged by the court who would rather have the parties resolve the matter themselves.

Once a settlement has been reached, each side executes a **release** which relieves the other side of any further rights or obligations in the matter. The parties then move to have the case dismissed based on the fact of the settlement. The court may order the matter dismissed either with or without prejudice. If the matter is dismissed with prejudice, the plaintiff may not re-institute the lawsuit at a later date. If the matter is dismissed without prejudice, the lawsuit may be re-instituted if the conditions of the settlement are not met. Furthermore, the parties may sue on the settlement agreement itself as a breach of contract case.

Example: *In the example mentioned above involving the car accident, because each side may be somewhat at fault, the parties agree to a settlement in which the defendant agrees only to pay a portion of the claimed damages. The defendant then moves to have the suit dismissed based on the settlement agreement.*

Ethical Concerns

Most of the ethical problems associated with an actual trial arise because of evidentiary practices of the litigants, a subject more appropriately discussed in an evidentiary text. However, even excluding evidentiary problems, there may be ethical concerns with the motions filed during and after the trial. Attorneys, and by extension their staffs, are precluded from filing frivolous motions by both the American Bar Association rules and the state of New York ethical statutes. Furthermore, there may be ethical problems with parties instituting frivolous lawsuits just in the hopes of forcing the opposing side to settle because the settlement would be less expensive than defending the frivolous action.

Chapter Review

Anytime after 40 days have elapsed after the service on the defendant, the plaintiff may file a notice of issue with the court to have the case placed on the court calendar for a trial date. In the notice of issue the plaintiff may make a jury demand, or the defendant may make its own jury demand. Only cases involving money damages or actions involving certain real estate problems are permitted to have a jury trial; all other actions are tried by the judge in a bench trial. In a bench trial, the court may utilize the advice of an advisory jury or a referee, but the ultimate decision still rests with the judge.

The parties select the jury from a jury panel, and in civil cases in New York the jury is composed of six members, with one or two alternates if so authorized by the court. The decision of the jury must be agreed to by at least five of the six jurors. The jury can render either a general verdict in which they simply indicate an ultimate conclusion, a special verdict in which they indicate the specific findings of facts on which they based their ultimate conclusions, or a general verdict accompanied by written questions. The jury retires to deliberate only after being instructed on the law by the judge.

During the trial either side may move for a directed verdict or a summary judgment which, if granted, terminates the proceedings. Both sides are also permitted to request specific jury instructions be given by the judge. After the verdict is rendered, the losing side may move for a new trial, reconsideration, or JNOV.

Once a decision has been rendered after a complete hearing, the matter is deemed to be res judicata with respect to the claims involved in the trial or collaterally estopped from being brought again if the issues determined in the earlier proceeding are identical to the issues raised in the later proceeding.

In all civil actions the parties themselves may reach their own agreement with respect to liability by settling the case, after which the action will be dismissed based on the parties' settlement.

Key Terms

Advisory jury – jury authorized by a judge in a bench trial to give advice to the judge

Bench trial – trial by judge

Collateral estoppel – doctrine that issues already determined may not be retried at a later date

Evidence log – method of keeping track of all evidence to be presented at trial

General verdict – verdict indicating only who is liable

General verdict accompanied by answers to interrogatories – verdict in which the jury responds to specific questions asked by the parties

Jury demand – procedure for requesting a jury trial

Motion for a new trial – posttrial motion based on irregularities in the proceedings

Motion for a judgment notwithstanding the verdict (JNOV) – request that the judge rule opposite to the jury findings

Motion for directed verdict – request that the judge tell the jury they must find for the moving party

Motion to reconsider – request to have the jury reconsider because the decision was not based on the weight of the evidence

Notice of issue – procedure for having the case placed on the court calendar

Peremptory challenge – right to exclude potential jurors for any reason

Pretrial conference – meeting with the litigants and the judge to limit trial issues

Referee – person appointed by the judge in a bench trial to advise the judge

Release – agreement entered into by parties to a lawsuit relieving each other of further liability

Res judicata – doctrine precluding the same claim being raised twice

Settlement – agreement between the parties to a lawsuit to terminate the suit

Special verdict – verdict in which the jury indicates specific findings of facts

Voir dire – name for the process of jury selection

Edited Judicial Decisions

In the Matter of the Guardianship and Custody of Julian P.H.
177 Misc. 2d 176 (Fam. 1998)

In this proceeding to terminate parental rights, respondent parents move for summary judgment dismissing the petition on the grounds: that the allegations supporting the cause of action (permanent neglect) were in issue and actually litigated in a prior recently concluded proceeding to extend the foster care placement of respondents' three children (*see*, Family Ct Act § *1055*[b]); that the court expressly found in the prior proceeding that permanent neglect does not exist; and that the New York City Commissioner of Social Services (hereinafter the Commissioner) and/or her agent, The Salvation Army (the authorized agency providing foster care services in this case), are now collaterally estopped from maintaining otherwise (*see*, *Matter of Suffolk County Dept. of Social Servs. v. James M.*, 83 NY2d 178 [1994]; *see also*, *Matter of Sara L.*, 249 AD2d 23). For the following reasons, the motion is granted.

I.

The prior proceeding to extend foster care placement was concluded after an extensive hearing. Over the course of seven days, the court heard the testimony of ten witnesses (including a court-appointed forensic expert) and received in evidence 37 exhibits (including comprehensive diagnostic and social work assessments on respondents and their three children). As mandated by Family Court Act § *1055*(b), the court carefully reviewed the entire history of the children's placement, the continued appropriateness of the court-ordered family service plan (designed to "encourage and strengthen the parental relationship," facilitate the rehabilitation of the family, and result in the children's discharge from foster care at the earliest time [*see*, Family. Ct. Act § *1055*(c); Social Services Law § *384-b*(1)(a); § 409-e]), and the extent to which respondents complied with that plan.

In detailed factual findings at the conclusion of the hearing, the court found, *inter alia*, that respondents had made "remarkable progress" in overcoming the problems which initially led to their children's foster care placement, that respondents had "visited the children continuously and ... maintained extremely close ties to them," and that respondents are now rehabilitated and competent parents.

At the hearing, the Commissioner opposed a return of the children to respondents' custody. Indeed, notwithstanding respondents' great progress, the Commissioner sought an order modifying the goal of the family service plan from "discharge to parent" to "freeing the children for adoption." It was in response to the Commissioner's application for such relief and based on the court's separate statutory obligation to determine respondents' compliance with the family service plan (Family Ct. Act § *1055*[b][iv][A][3]) that the court made the factual findings at issue and concluded that grounds to terminate parental rights do not exist. Thus, the court ordered a trial discharge of two of respondents' children, to be followed shortly thereafter by the trial discharge of the third and continued supervision of respondents by the Commissioner's caseworkers.

II.

The doctrine of collateral estoppel bars the relitigation of factual issues between the same parties when those issues were in controversy and actually determined in a prior lawsuit. (*Kaufman v. Eli Lilly & Co.*, 65 NY2d 449 [1985].) That the parties did not intend to be bound by the factual findings in the prior litigation does not preclude the application of collateral estoppel. (*Matter of American Ins. Co. [Messinger]*, 43 NY2d 184 [1977].) All that is necessary is that (i) there be an "identity of issues" that necessarily were decided in the prior litigation and are decisive of the present litigation, and (ii) the party against whom collateral estoppel is sought had a "full and fair" opportunity to be heard. (*Kaufman v. Eli Lilly & Co., supra,* at 456; *Schwartz v. Public Adm'r. of County of Bronx*, 24 NY2d 65 [1969].)

The material factual claims at issue in the present proceeding to terminate parental rights, (i.e., whether respondents planned adequately for and maintained sufficient contact with their children) [*see*, Family Ct Act § *614*; Social Services Law § *384-b*(3), (4)(d)], necessarily were at issue and decided in the prior proceeding the Commissioner filed to extend foster care placement (*see*, point I, *supra*). As such, an "identity of issues" exists, and the Commissioner indisputably had a "full and fair" opportunity to be heard. The doctrine of collateral estoppel, therefore, is applicable as a matter of law.

Further, the children's best interests and principles of judicial economy require a proper application of collateral estoppel so as to obtain a prompt determination of litigation involving the children's foster care placement. (*See*, *Matter of Sanjivini K.*, 40 NY2d 1025, 1027 [1976] [emphasizing that courts should consolidate and expeditiously decide proceedings affecting children in foster care]; *see also*, *Matter of Dutchess County Dept. of Social Servs. [Mark M.]*, 196 AD2d 196 [2d Dept 1994] [Per Curiam] [stressing that the Family Court should make every effort promptly to resolve proceedings concerning the custody of children]; *cf.*, Social Services Law § *383*[5].) Here, the Commissioner's desire to relitigate factual issues previously decided and involving the testimony of the same ten witnesses simply because the Commissioner disagrees with the court's prior findings would result in inordinate delay, waste limited judicial resources and do nothing to advance the children's interests. The Commissioner's appropriate remedy is to seek appellate review of the prior findings.

In view of the foregoing, summary judgment dismissing the present petition to terminate parental rights is required.

Siriano v. Beth Israel Hospital Center
161 Misc. 2d 512 (1994)

During jury selection the six codefendants have used their peremptory challenges to excuse all nine minority venire persons (six black and three Latino) who have to date been examined. Plaintiffs assert that this exclusion has been impermissibly based on race and request judicial relief.

FACTS

The plaintiff Joseph Siriano, a white of Italian ancestry, asserts that he was injured in a construction accident and has instituted this action against the owner of premises where the accident occurred and five contractors and subcontractors.

Justice Helen Freedman granted each defendant three peremptory challenges and gave plaintiffs nine challenges. As of March 16, when an application was made to me, two jurors (both white) had been seated. Plaintiffs had exercised five challenges (four white and one black) while defendants jointly exercised 11 challenges (the nine referred to above as well as two whites). In addition the parties jointly excused approximately 180 prospective jurors, the vast majority of whom were apparently excused due to problems resulting from the stated length of the trial. No breakdown of the racial composition of these persons was available.

In the afternoon of March 16, plaintiffs' counsel complained of the actions of the defendants in excusing all of the minority jurors. After hearing argument, I determined that the statistics displayed a *prima facie* case of racial discrimination and directed defendants to offer race neutral explanations for their challenges. On the following two afternoons I heard defendants' explanations for the exercise of their challenges and examined, together with counsel, the three minority jurors (two black and one Latina) who were then available.

DISCUSSION

In *Swain v. Alabama* (380 U.S. 202 [1965]), it was held that purposeful exclusion of blacks from juries violates the Equal Protection Clause, but proof was required that the prosecutor had followed such a pattern in cases other than the one before the court. This formulation was found unworkable and was therefore rejected in *Batson v. Kentucky* (476 U.S. 79 [1986]), where it was held that "a defendant may establish a *prima facie* case of purposeful discrimination in selection of the petit jury solely on evidence concerning the prosecutor's exercise of peremptory challenges at the defendant's trial" (at 96). The Court ruled that to "establish such a case, the defendant first must show that he is a member of a cognizable racial group ... and that the prosecutor has exercised peremptory challenges to remove from the venire members of the defendant's race ... [and that the] facts and any other relevant circumstances raise an inference that the prosecutor used that practice to exclude the veniremen from the petit jury on account of their race" (at 96). As an example it was stated that a " 'pattern' of strikes against black jurors included in the particular venire might give rise to an inference of discrimination," and that once there is a "*prima facie* showing, the burden shifts to the State to come forward with a neutral explanation for challenging black jurors, [and the] trial court then will have the duty to determine if the defendant has established purposeful discrimination" (at 97–98).

Although in 1993 the First Department in *People v. Doran* (195 AD2d 364) restated the foregoing requirements, including the necessity of showing that the prosecutor removed "members of [the] defendant's race from the panel" (at 365), it was held in *Powers v. Ohio* (499 U.S. 400 [1991]), that a juror has a constitutional right not to be excluded from a jury on account of race and a defendant of a different race "can raise the third-party equal protection claims of jurors excluded by the prosecution because of their race" (at 415).

Two months after the decision in *Powers (supra)*, in *Edmonson v. Leesville Concrete Co.* (500 U.S. 614 [1991]), it was announced that the harms recognized in Powers are not limited to the criminal sphere, and that courts must entertain a challenge to a private litigant's racially discriminatory use of peremptory challenges in a civil trial, concluding that it would be left to the trial courts in the first instance to develop evidentiary rules for implementing the decision. Although many courts have dealt with this issue in criminal cases, there are very few decisions in the civil area, with no reported case having been located in New York.

Coming to the action at bar, the explanations for the exercise of peremptory challenges offered by defendants predominately involved concerns because the jurors, members of their family or close friends had at some time been injured in an accident (Smith, Walker, Flores, Cypher, Allen and Stubblefield). Some of the other partial explanations offered as to the following prospective jurors were: (Rosario) two young jurors had already been selected and a third young juror would not provide a desired mix; (Stubblefield) father had died at Beth Israel Hospital, a defendant herein, although no fault was ascribed by the juror to the hospital; (Guzman) three brothers were in the construction trade; (Smith) wife works in the medical records room at Presbyterian Hospital.

The three jurors who were examined by counsel and the court (Smith, Walker and Guzman) appeared to be sensible, intelligent persons, who all stated that they could and would fairly try the action, for which promise I could see no valid reason to question.

After having heard from the aforesaid three jurors and the submissions and arguments of counsel, I now have to decide whether to deprive defendants of their exercised peremptory challenges granted by CPLR § 4109, which challenges normally permit a party to excuse a juror without offering a reason. Such challenges are not constitutionally protected fundamental rights, but rather are state-created means of achieving an impartial jury (*Georgia v. McCollum*, 505 U.S. ___, 112 S. Ct. 2348 [1992]). The determination of this issue, as indicated above, depends on whether these defendants have exercised their challenges in a purposefully discriminatory manner. The question poses great difficulty for a Trial Judge. As noted by Judge Bellacosa in his concurring opinion (on behalf of Chief Judge Wachtler and Judge Titone) in *People v. Bolling* (79 NY2d 317 [1992]), "[a]nalytically, peremptories and race-neutral articulations present a quintessential and untenable dualism" (at 326). In that opinion the three Judges urged, as did Justice Marshall in his concurring opinion in *Batson (supra),* the elimination of the peremptory challenge process, stating that it now produces "a seemingly endless variety of issues and permutations, manifesting the intractable struggle of the lower courts to implement the unmanageable and self-contradictory Batson remedy, [and that it] has become virtually impossible for appellate courts or trial courts to discern proper gradations and variations and to provide meaningful procedural guidance guaranteeing some measure of consistent application" (at 329).

In deciding the present issue, I must observe that I am aware of a general perception of lawyers involved in the personal injury field of a preference of plaintiff's counsel for minority jurors and an opposite preference of defense counsel. These preferences are, of course, not true of all counsel, nor in all situations. But this general perception is reflected in the numerous venue motions wherein plaintiffs seek a trial in Bronx County (where there is more likely to be a minority jury), whereas defendants are likely to oppose such a trial location.

Although I do not in any manner doubt that the attorneys for the defendants in asserting the challenges aforesaid believed that they were acting in the best interests of their respective clients and were not intentionally racist, the impact of their actions, resulting in the elimination to date of all minority jurors, has had a discriminatory impact. As noted in Batson, "[c]ircumstantial evidence of invidious intent may include proof of disproportionate impact ... [and that] under some circumstances proof of discriminatory impact 'may for all practical purposes demonstrate unconstitutionality because in various circumstances the discrimination is very difficult to explain on nonracial grounds' " (476 U.S. 79, 93, *supra*).

Just as it is impermissible to eliminate blacks from a jury "on the assumption that they will be biased in a particular case simply because the defendant is black" (*Batson v. Kentucky, supra,* at 97), it is improper to exclude them from a jury because of a general perception that it is likely that they may be more sympathetic to an injured plaintiff.

In view of all of the evidence before me, I find that there has been a purposeful discrimination against the minority jurors excused and I therefore direct that to the extent that they are still available, the three examined jurors (Smith, Walker and Guzman) be seated together with the two jurors previously selected, and that jury selection continue. (*See*, *People v. Frye*, 191 AD2d 581 [2d Dept. 1993], where the Court permitted the retention of jurors seated prior to the day the discriminatory pattern was revealed; *People v. Mitchell*, 80 NY2d 519, 530 [1992], where it was held that a Batson claim was sustained because "the exclusion of even a single juror on racial grounds is constitutionally forbidden.")

Exercises

1. Go to the library and review the Pattern Jury Instructions for the state of New York.

2. Why does the American legal system have the doctrines of res judicata and collateral estoppel? Explain.

3. Why do the courts favor settlements? Explain.

4. Differentiate between a motion for a directed verdict and a motion for a JNOV.

5. Give several reasons why a litigant would want to exclude potential jurors.

Chapter Seven

JUDGMENTS AND APPEALS

Introduction

Once the trial has been completed and a verdict has been rendered, either of the parties may be dissatisfied with the result. If the litigant is dissatisfied, he or she may appeal the decision to a higher court, either to the Appellate Term or the Appellate Division, which, as was discussed in Chapter One, provides an intermediate review of the trial court's decision. If still dissatisfied, the parties may appeal again to the New York Court of Appeals.

At the conclusion of the appeals process, or if no appeal is taken, the victorious party may need to have the decision of the court enforced against the party who was found liable. Unfortunately, many losing litigants do not immediately accede to the final decision of the court, and consequently the "winner" must seek to have the judgment against the "loser" enforced by following the enforcement procedures specified in the CPLR.

This chapter will concentrate on this aspect of the conclusion of the litigation process in the appeal and enforcement of judgments. The paralegal serves several functions in aiding the attorney in these processes. For the appeal, the paralegal may be assigned the task of researching the appropriate law upon which the appeal may be based, and to draft the initial version of the brief that the attorney will submit to the court for its consideration. With respect to the enforcement of judgments, the paralegal will be required to complete and file all necessary forms, assist in locating assets of the obligor that can be attached, and help determine the appropriate amount for the allocation of costs.

Appellate Procedure

If a litigant wishes to take an appeal, he or she must note the appeal within 30 days after he or she is served with

- a copy of the order of judgment of the trial court
- written notice of the entry of the judgment. CPLR § 5513.

As a general rule, the time period cannot be extended, but the court does have the ability to extend the period only in the following circumstances pursuant to section 5514 of the CPLR:

- An alternate method for appeal is available and an original notice was dismissed.
- The attorney who handled the case became disabled.
- There was an error made by the court, the appellant was a transferee of the litigant's interest, or some formal omission inadvertently occurred.

<u>Example</u>: *The trial court found for the defendant and the plaintiff wishes to appeal. The defendant enters the judgment in his favor to the court and serves the plaintiff with notice of the entry of the judgment on November 1. The appeal must be filed by November 31; however, on the 20th of November the plaintiff's attorney dies. In this instance the court may grant an extension of the time in which to note the appeal if it can be shown that the deceased attorney's office could not prepare the documents in time.*

The party who takes the appeal is called the **appellant**, and the party who must respond to the appeal is called the **appellee**. Appeals are classified either as "by right" or "by permission."

Appeal by Right

A party may appeal to the Appellate Division any final interlocutory judgment of the supreme or county court, except for an Article 78 proceeding, and motions for a more definite statement or a motion to strike. CPLR § 3024(a) (*see* Chapter One).

<u>Example</u>: *In a breach of contract suit the plaintiff wishes to introduce evidence of the value of the loss of goodwill. The defendant moves to exclude this evidence, and the trial court grants the motion. The plaintiff may appeal this decision to the Appellate Division.*

A final order of the Appellate Division can be appealed if

- there is a dissent by two judges on a stated question of law
- the Appellate Division construed the New York or United States Constitution in reaching its decision.

If the cause of action is based on a constitutional question, the final decision of the trial court may be immediately appealed to the Court of Appeals without the necessity of the intermediate appeal. Intermediate orders of the trial court on an earlier appeal to the Appellate Division may also be directly appealed to the Court of Appeals.

<u>Example</u>: *A plaintiff contends that a city ordinance violates her rights under the due process clause of the Constitution. When the trial court eventually renders its judgment, the matter may be directly appealed to the Court of Appeals without first going to the Appellate Division.*

Appeal by Permission

A party may appeal any trial court order to the Appellate Division with the permission of the trial judge or a judge of the Appellate Division. A litigant may appeal to the Court of Appeals by permission of the Court of Appeals or the Appellate Division if the order being appealed is not one that permits an appeal by right or concerns an Article 78 proceeding. To be granted leave to appeal to the Court of Appeals the potential appellant must acquire the consent of two of the justices. CPLR § 5602(a). Furthermore, the Appellate Division may grant an *ex parte* motion denied by the supreme or county court.

The appellee has the right to note a cross-appeal by filing a notice of cross-appeal within ten days after service of the notice of appeal, or 30 days after entry and notice, whichever is longer.

Example: *A litigant has sought a mandamus proceeding against a state official* (see *Chapter Eight) and an order has been entered against her. She may seek an appeal to the Court of Appeals if she can convince two of the justices of the Court of Appeals to grant her request.*

Stay Pending Appeal

Once the trial court has entered its decision, the losing party becomes obligated to meet the requirements of the verdict; however, if an appeal is taken, the party may want to delay the obligation until the appellate court has ruled because the appellate court may find in the obligor's favor. Under these circumstances, the obligor may seek a **stay of execution** if the following requirements are met:

- The obligor obtains a stipulation to that effect from the obligee.
- The obligor posts a bond with the court. A **bond** is money or other property that is held by the court to ensure that the party will be able to meet the obligation if he or she eventually is unsuccessful in the appeal.
- The obligor obtains an order from the court to stay the execution of the judgment.

If a stay of execution is ordered, the stay remains in effect until five days after the appeal is concluded with either an order of affirmation or modification. If a subsequent appeal is taken within this five-day period, the stay of execution remains in effect until the conclusion of the ultimate appeal. If an ultimate appeal is made, but denied, the stay remains in effect until five days after service of the order of denial.

Example: *A trial court finds for the plaintiff in the amount of $150,000. The defendant wants to appeal and wants to avoid paying the money in case the appellate court reverses the trial court's verdict. The defendant files a motion to stay execution of the judgment, and the* *trial court grants the motion. The defendant must now post a bond with the court with property valued at the full amount of the judgment—$150,000.*

The Appeal

In an appeal, unlike a trial, there is no jury and the matter is decided by a panel of appellate judges. The appellate court does not retry facts, but only determines questions of law raised during the trial procedure and verdict.

The appeal consists of the submission to the court by both parties of an appellate brief that contains a statement of the facts, indicates the issues of law raised by the facts, the legal arguments of each side, and the prayer for relief. Both parties receive the opposite side's brief before the hearing.

At the hearing, no witnesses are called nor is any evidence presented. The counsel for each side is permitted a specified period of time in which to argue the case orally and answer questions posed by the judges. The eventual decision of the judges is published, and it becomes part of the common law of New York State. The ultimate decision of the appellate court may take one of the following forms

- *Affirm*. The appellate court upholds the decision of the trial court.
- *Reverse*. The appellate court decides against the trial court's decision.
- *Modify*. The appellate court makes some change to the decision of the trial court.
- *Reversed and Remanded*. The appellate court reverses the trial court's decision and sends the matter back to the trial court to retry the case following the dictates of the appellate court.

Enforcement of Judgments

Once a final judgment has been rendered and all appeals are complete or none are filed within the statutory period, the victorious party can make a motion to the court for execution of the judgment if the obligor fails to fulfill the judgment obligation. The moving party must include a list of the obligor's property to be used for the execution, but the following assets are exempt from the execution:

- the household exemption; however, these goods may not be exempt if they were used as a security for a loan to the obligor
- the homestead exemption, including the house and land up to a value of $10,000
- damages resulting from injuries to the exempt property
- trust corpus for which the obligor is the main beneficiary
- security deposits
- ninety percent of the obligor's income
- earnings from service in the Armed Forces.

The court clerk or the judgment creditor's attorney can issue a restraining notice so that the obligor cannot transfer assets before execution. Further, a special proceeding is required against any third person who possesses the obligor's property.

Example: The obligor has loaned his cousin a painting worth $10,000. In order to help the obligor, the cousin refuses to relinquish the painting for execution. The creditor may initiate proceedings against the cousin to attach the property.

The actual execution is done by the sheriff of the county in which the property is located, as soon as the sheriff receives the order of execution from the court clerk or the creditor's attorney. The execution must be returned within 60 days. Once the sheriff **levies** the property, it is sold at public auction. If the proceeds from the sale of the asset exceed the judgment, the obligor receives the excess. If the sheriff finds the property unsalable, he or she must obtain the consent of the court to destroy or otherwise dispose of the property. Attachment of income is limited to $25 a week.

<u>Example</u>: *To satisfy a judgment, the creditor has the sheriff levy against the obligor's mobile home. The judgment was for $7,500. At auction, the mobile home sells for $35,000. The obligor receives $27,500, less costs, after the sale.*

There are certain rules for particular types of judgments:

Real Property Judgments

To execute against realty, the creditor must describe the property with particularity in the order of execution, using the exact description of the property as it appears on the deed filed with the county recorder's office.

Small Claims Judgments

The Small Claims Court may award treble damages if

- the judgment results from the obligor's regular course of business or from repeated transactions with the creditor
- there are at least three other unsatisfied judgments against the obligor
- the obligor fails to satisfy the latest judgment within 30 days.

Any fees associated with execution of the judgment are added to the levy.

Sister State and Foreign Country Judgments

The execution of foreign judgments is covered by Article 54 of the CPLR. In order to execute and levy property located in New York based on a foreign (sister state) judgment, the judgment creditor must file the execution in the county clerk's office in the county where the property to be levied against is located. Once the note is filed, it becomes an order, but the filing will be vacated if the foreign judgment is reversed or modified on appeal. The judgment creditor must mail notice to the obligor within 30 days of filing, and the actual execution is delayed for 30 days after the judgment creditor files proof of service on the obligor. Every state court is required under the U.S. Constitution to give full faith and credit to sister state judgments, provided that

- the foreign court had jurisdiction over the parties
- the foreign judgment is a final judgment
- the foreign judgment was "on the merits."

<u>Example</u>: *A New Jersey resident sues another New Jersey resident on a contract debt, and the trial court finds for the plaintiff. The plaintiff cannot locate any the defendant's assets in New Jersey, but knows of two bank accounts the defendant maintains in New York banks. The plaintiff can take the final order of the trial court and file it for execution with the county clerks' office in the New York county in which the bank accounts are maintained. Because the New Jersey court had jurisdiction over the parties, there was a full trial, and the judgment is final (absent an appeal), the New York court will give full faith and credit to the New Jersey judgment.*

The obligor under a sister state judgment may assert the following defenses in an effort to prevent New York from enforcing the foreign judgment:

- The foreign court lacked jurisdiction.
- The obligor did not appear in the foreign court.
- The judgment is not a final judgment.
- The judgment was not reached on the merits.

Despite the requirement of full faith and credit, the New York courts exclude from execution the following judgments:

- tax judgments
- penal judgments

- judgments that run contrary to New York public policy
- foreign land judgments
- judgments subject to equitable defenses in the sister state
- judgments that are deemed to be "inconsistent" (determined on a case-by-case basis).

Judgments from courts of foreign nations are not afforded the constitutional guarantees of full faith and credit, but New York has passed the **Uniform Foreign Money Judgment Recognition Act** which provides the statutory basis for New York courts to enforce foreign country judgments.

Interests, Costs, and Disbursements

In addition to the actual damages awarded by the trial court, the successful party may also be entitled to certain interest payments on the award and certain enumerated costs.

Interest

Interest is permitted to be assessed for contract and property damage awards and wrongful death actions from the time of the injury until the verdict, but this pre-verdict interest is not permitted in personal injury actions. The successful party is entitled to receive interest on the award from the verdict date until ultimate payment.

Costs

A plaintiff is denied costs if he or she originally filed the suit in a higher court when the matter could—and should—have been brought before a lesser court of original jurisdiction.

<u>Example</u>: *In order to bring an action in the Supreme Court, a plaintiff alleges damages of $35,000. At trial it is determined that the plaintiff's damages are $20,000 at most and there was no rational basis for alleging a greater amount except to invoke the jurisdiction of the*

supreme court rather than the county court. In this instance, the court will probably disallow costs.

To obtain costs, the successful party must make a motion to the court. However, if the court determines that the lawsuit represented frivolous litigation, costs are assessed in favor of the defendant, with attorney's fees up to a maximum of $10,000. CPLR § 8303-a. Furthermore, the court has the discretion to impose sanctions against the plaintiff in a frivolously brought action up to an additional $10,000.

As a general rule, attorney's fees are not recoverable unless expressly agreed to by contract between the parties or authorized by the statute on which the lawsuit is based. The following items are assessable as costs:

- witness fees, reporters' fees, etc.
- costs of taking depositions
- publication fees (when publication was permitted by the court)
- costs of certified copies of papers necessarily obtained for trial
- costs of copying opening and jury charges
- other printing costs
- fees for entering and docketing the case
- sheriff's fees for execution of judgment
- costs for transcripts of the testimony taken at the EBT, not to exceed $250
- costs of subpoenas
- expenses incurred to stay enforcement of judgment
- other expenses the court deems reasonable and necessary.

Ethical Concerns

Ethical considerations can affect both parties to the lawsuit. It is considered to be unethical to file frivolous lawsuits simply to coerce a defendant into settlement, and it is equally unethical to hide assets or refuse to pay judgments just to frustrate the successful party in the hopes that he or she will not go through with the execution process, especially if the award is relatively small. Furthermore, it is equally unethical to initiate the appellate process just to delay ultimate execution of the judgment.

Chapter Review

Once a verdict has been reached by the court of original jurisdiction, the unsuccessful party may note an appeal within 30 days of the final order being entered. The court enforces this time limit fairly strictly and permits extensions only in very limited circumstances. A party may appeal either by right or with permission of the court.

An appellate court, after reading the parties' written memoranda of law and hearing their oral arguments, may either affirm the lower court's judgment, modify the judgment, reverse the judgment, or remand the judgment for further proceedings at the trial level consistent with the appellate court's ruling. If still dissatisfied, the unsuccessful party on appeal may still appeal the matter to the highest court in New York, the New York Court of Appeals. Pending the appeal, the judgment obligor can stay the execution of the judgment by moving for a stay and posting a bond with the court.

Once the decision is final and all appeals have been exhausted, the successful party can execute judgment against the obligor by filing the final order with the sheriff in the county where the obligor has non-exempt property. The sheriff will then levy this property for sale at public auction. The successful party may also be entitled to receive interest and costs in addition to the actual award.

Key Terms

Affirm – uphold a lower court's decision

Appeal – review of a judicial decision to a higher court

Appellant – person who brings the appeal

Appellee – person who defends against the appeal

Bond – property given to the court to ensure that the judgment can be paid

Cross-appeal – appellee's appeal against the appellant

Modify – amend the decision of a lower court

Remand – send the case back to the lower court

Reverse – change the decision of the lower court

Stay of execution – order permitting the obligor to wait to pay the judgment until after the appeal

Uniform Foreign Money Judgment Recognition Act – statute passed by New York to enforce money judgments of foreign courts

Edited Judicial Decisions

Burke v. Crosson, as Chief Administrator of the Courts of the State of New York
85 NY2d 10 (1995)

Plaintiffs, three Onondaga County Court Judges, commenced this action, *inter alia*, to challenge the disparity that exists between their salary and the salary of their counterparts in 13 other counties. Defendants seek appellate review of a Supreme Court decision that dismissed most of plaintiffs' claims but granted them summary judgment on their first cause of action. The critical threshold issue on this appeal by defendants from the final Supreme Court judgment awarding attorney's fees is whether, in a prior appeal, the Appellate Division erred in declining to consider the merits of this determination on the ground that it was embodied in an earlier judgment that was final and therefore not reviewable under CPLR § 5501(a)(1). We now hold that the Appellate Division misapprehended the principles governing the finality of judgments and that, accordingly, its refusal to review the issue defendants proffered was an error.

A brief summary of this case's procedural history is necessary to an understanding of the finality problem its facts present. Plaintiffs' complaint for declaratory and monetary relief set forth 16 causes of action, all relating to the difference between plaintiffs' salaries and the higher salaries paid to County Court Judges in other counties. A 17th cause of action concerned the difference between plaintiffs' salaries and the salaries paid to Court of Claims Judges. The gist of plaintiffs' complaint was that the pay discrepancies violated their constitutional rights to equal protection because there was no rational economic or judicial basis for the disparate treatment. In addition to seeking a favorable declaration, plaintiffs' complaint sought a judgment for back pay retroactive to October 1, 1978, and an incidental award of attorney's fees under 42 USC § 1988.

The Supreme Court agreed with plaintiffs that the discrepancy between their salaries and those of Albany County Court Judges was not rationally based. Accordingly, on November 15, 1991, the Supreme Court granted plaintiffs' motion for summary judgment on their first cause of action and awarded them the back pay they sought. The court also granted plaintiffs counsel fees pursuant to 42 USC § 1988, but it postponed assessment of the amount pending a hearing. Plaintiffs' 16 other causes of action were dismissed as either moot or lacking in substantive merit.

Plaintiffs appealed from the Supreme Court's dismissal of their remaining 16 causes of action. Defendants, however, did not take a cross-appeal at that time. Instead, they proceeded directly to the hearing in which the question of the amount of attorney's fees was to be litigated. Following that hearing, the trial court awarded $13,125 in attorney's fees and a judgment for that amount was entered against defendants on May 7, 1992. Defendants then took an appeal from that judgment, asserting that the appeal brought up for review the Supreme Court's November 15, 1991, order disposing of the pay disparity issue.

The Appellate Division simultaneously decided both parties' appeals. On plaintiffs' appeal, the Appellate Division affirmed the result in the Supreme Court, concluding that the dismissal of 16 of the 17 causes of action was proper. Additionally, it held that the November 15, 1991, disposition against defendants was a "final" judgment under the doctrine of implied severance and that it therefore "cannot be brought up for review on appeal from the [subsequent] order [assessing attorney's fees]" (191 AD2d 997, 998, *citing Crystal v. Manes*, 130 AD2d 979; *Acres v. Hitchcock*, 77 AD2d 744). That view was also implicitly incorporated into the Court's decision on defendants' appeal from the attorney-fee award, in which the Appellate Division reversed and remitted for further proceedings on the attorney-fee assessment question alone without addressing the merits of the underlying determination on the pay disparity question.

On remand, Supreme Court reduced plaintiffs' attorney's fees award to $9,185.69, and judgment to that effect was entered on January 20, 1994. Defendants then successfully moved this Court for leave to appeal from this judgment (denominated an "order"), seeking review of "so much of the prior nonfinal [Appellate Division] order ... as affirmed [the] nonfinal order of Supreme Court, entered November 15, 1991 ... granting plaintiffs summary judgment on their first cause of action and awarding back pay." Defendants' appeal requires us to decide the correctness of the Appellate Division's threshold determination that review of the November 15, 1991, Supreme Court disposition was not authorized by CPLR § 5501(a)(1), the reviewability provision applicable to defendants' appeal.

Under CPLR § 5501(a)(1), an appeal from a final judgment brings up for review "any nonfinal judgment or order which necessarily affects the final judgment ... provided that such nonfinal judgment or order has not previously been reviewed by the court to which the appeal is taken." Since this provision authorizes review only of prior judgments and orders that are nonfinal, the classification of a particular judgment or order as final or nonfinal is critical to the statute's proper application. We note that, contrary to plaintiffs' argument here, the concept of finality as used in CPLR § 5501(a)(1) is identical to the concept of finality that is routinely used to analyze appealability under article VI, § 3(b)(1), (2) and (6) of the State Constitution and the related statutory provisions (*see*, CPLR §§ 5601, 5602).

The concept of finality is a complex one that cannot be exhaustively defined in a single phrase, sentence or writing (*see generally*, Cohen and Karger, *Powers of the New York Court of Appeals* § 9, at 39; Scheinkman, *The Civil Jurisdiction of the New York Court of Appeals: The Rule and Role of Finality*, 54 St. John's L. Rev. 443). Nonetheless, a fair working definition of the concept can be stated as follows: a "final" order or judgment is one that disposes of all of the causes of action between the parties in the action or proceeding and leaves nothing for further judicial action apart from mere ministerial matters (*see generally*, Cohen and Karger, op. cit., § 10, 11). Under this definition, an order or judgment that disposes of some but not all of the substantive and monetary disputes between the same parties is, in most cases, nonfinal. Thus, a nonfinal order or judgment results when a court decides one or more but not all causes of action in the complaint against a particular defendant or where the court disposes of a counterclaim or affirmative defense but leaves other causes of action between the same parties for resolution in further judicial proceedings (*see, e.g., Marna Constr. Corp. v. Town of Huntington*, 31 NY2d 854).

An exception to these general principles exists in situations where the causes of action or counterclaims that have been resolved may be deemed to be "impliedly severed" from those that have been left pending. Where implied severance is available, the order resolving a cause of action or counterclaim is treated as a final one for purposes of determining its appealability or reviewability.

The "implied severance" doctrine has had a checkered history and our past articulations of the rule have been somewhat difficult to reconcile (*see, e.g., Associated Coal Sales Corp. v. Hughes*, 46 NY2d 1071; *Orange & Rockland Utils. v. Howard Oil Co.*, 46 NY2d 880; *Ratka v. St. Francis Hosp.*, 44 NY2d 604; *Lizza Indus. v. Long Is. Light. Co.*, 36 NY2d 754; *Behren v. Papworth*, 30 NY2d 532; *Rose v. Bailey*, 28 NY2d 857; *Kelly v. Bremmerman*, 21 NY2d 195; *Sirlin Plumbing Co. v. Maple Hill Homes*, 20 NY2d 401). However, as may be discerned from a close review of our contemporary decisions on the point, the "implied severance" doctrine has now evolved into a very limited exception to the general rule of nonfinality.

Under this approach to implied severance, an order that disposes of some but not all of the causes of action asserted in a litigation between parties may be deemed final under the doctrine of implied severance only if the causes of action it resolves do not arise out of the same transaction or continuum of facts or out of the same legal relationship as the unresolved causes of action (*see, Heller v. State of New York*, 81 NY2d 60, 62, n. 1; *Lizza Indus. v. Long Is. Light. Co., supra*). Thus, for example, an order dismissing or granting relief on one or more causes of action arising out of a single contract or series of factually related contracts would not be impliedly severable and would not be deemed final where other claims or counterclaims derived from the same contract or contracts were left pending. Similarly, where a negligence cause of action has been dismissed but there remain other claims for relief based on the same transaction or transactions, the doctrine of implied severance is not available, even though the underlying legal theories may be very different. Finally, implied severance is not applied where the court's order "decides some issues of relief but leaves pending between the same parties other such issues[, thereby] in effect divid[ing] a single cause of action" (*Sontag v. Sontag*, 66 NY2d 554, 555).

Viewed against these principles, the November 15, 1991, order granting plaintiffs summary judgment on their first cause of action and dismissing the others cannot be deemed final. Although all of the substantive issues between the parties were resolved, the order was facially nonfinal, since it left pending the assessment of attorney's fees—a matter that plainly required further judicial action of a nonministerial nature.

Moreover, implied severance was not available under these facts as a means of converting that facially nonfinal order to a theoretically final one. The resolved causes of action for declaratory and monetary relief were based on the same continuum of facts as the unresolved 42 USC § 1988 attorney-fee claim, (i.e., the enactment of a judicial salary scheme) that, in plaintiffs' view, violated their right to equal protection of the laws. Without that legislative act and the surrounding circumstances that plaintiffs allege rendered the act unlawful, there was no predicate for either a substantive cause of action or a claim for the attorney's fees incurred in vindicating plaintiffs' rights.

Indeed, plaintiffs' request for attorney's fees was made in the form of a demand for "costs," which was included in the boilerplate portion of the complaint seeking "[s]uch other, further and different relief which the Court may deem just and proper." As such, the request for attorney's fees was an integral part of each of the asserted causes of action rather than a separate cause of action of its own. It has previously been said that a request for back pay and a request for attorney's fees arising from the same wrong are "but a single cause of action" and that "one cannot divide a single cause of action" by "dividing the damage" in this manner (*Manko v. City of Buffalo*, 294 N.Y. 109, 111). So too, in this case—where plaintiffs have asserted 17 causes of action based on the same legislative enactment and have requested attorney's fees as an item of damages integral to each of those causes of action—the pending request for attorney's fees could not have been divided from the otherwise resolved causes of action and implied severance was necessarily unavailable (*Sontag v. Sontag, supra*).

Inasmuch as the November 15, 1991, order was not final and was not capable of being made final under the doctrine of implied severance, it should have been treated as a prior "nonfinal" order subject to review on plaintiffs' appeal from the final May 7, 1992, judgment pursuant to CPLR § 5501(a)(1). Further, since the order presents a question of law and CPLR § 5501(a)(1) also applies to the reviewability of prior orders in this Court, the correctness of the November 15, 1991, order is technically before us on this appeal. We conclude, however, that under the circumstances a remittal to the Appellate Division for a review of the order's underlying merits is the better course.

The Supreme Court granted plaintiffs summary judgment on the theory that there was no rational basis for paying them less than their counterparts in Albany County are paid. This determination was based on the relative equivalence of the cost of living in the two counties, as well as the similarities in the County Court Judges' caseloads and duties. In finding these factors dispositive, Supreme Court rejected defendants' contention that it was rational to pay Onondaga County Court Judges less than their Albany County peers because the cost of purchasing a home is significantly greater in Albany County than in Onondaga County. The correctness of the Supreme Court's determination depends, at least in part, on an analysis of the legal significance of the detailed facts set forth in the parties' submissions. It also rests on an understanding of regional economic conditions and local judicial practices. The case should thus be remitted for the Appellate Division's consideration of the pay disparity question.

Accordingly, the judgment of Supreme Court appealed from and the order of the Appellate Division brought up for review should be reversed and the case remitted to the Appellate Division for further proceedings in accordance with this opinion.

Intercontinental Credit Corporation Division of Pan American Trade Development Corp. v. Roth
78 NY2d 306 (1991)

On June 13, 1991, this Court dismissed as untimely a motion by defendant for leave to appeal (78 NY2d 909). By notice of motion served July 12, 1991, defendant moved for reargument, contending that the Court misapprehended the nature of the relief he sought. Plaintiff then cross-moved for sanctions pursuant to part 130 of the Rules of the Chief Administrator of the Courts (22 NYCRR 130-1.1 *et. seq.*), alleging that defendant's reargument motion was frivolous and made solely to delay the progress of enforcement proceedings pending against defendant in Israel. For the reasons that follow, defendant's motion for reargument should be denied and plaintiff's cross motion for sanctions granted.

Defendant's initial motion invoking CPLR § 5514's special extension for attorney disability was wholly without basis in the statute. The present motion is premised on a claim that we mistakenly treated the initial motion as one for leave to appeal rather than as one for permission to make such a motion "out of time." That claim, similarly, is frivolous. The utter lack of merit in these motions and the virtual impossibility of affecting the final judgment at this late stage in the litigation confirm plaintiff-cross-movant's contention that this reargument motion was made primarily to delay enforcement of a judgment in Israel. Indeed, although defendant has disputed plaintiff's characterizations of some of the background facts, he has made no more than a token effort to defend the merits of the present motion. Thus, his papers raise no significant issues requiring a further inquiry (*see*, 22 NYCRR 130-1.1[d]).

It is clear that the present motion was "undertaken primarily to delay or prolong" the Israeli enforcement proceedings (*see*, 22 NYCRR 130-1.1[c][2]). This is precisely the type of misuse of judicial process that part 130 was adopted to curtail. In imposing a sanction on both defendant and his attorney, we have considered the facts that plaintiff has been inappropriately hampered in its efforts to enforce a valid judgment, that this was defendant's second misguided effort to invoke the jurisdiction of this Court for purposes essentially unrelated to the legitimate settlement of controversies and that a specific, well-founded request for sanctions against both defendant and his counsel has been made (*cf., Matter of Minister, Elders & Deacons of Refm. Prot. Dutch Church v. 198 Broadway*, 76 NY2d 411, 414–415).

Accordingly, defendant's motion for reargument should be denied; a sanction in the amount of $2,500 should be imposed on defendant Henry Roth, a separate sanction in the amount of $2,500 should be imposed on his attorney, Louis H. Benjamin, and plaintiff's cross motion should otherwise be denied.

Motion for reargument of motion for leave to appeal denied. Cross-motion for imposition of sanctions granted and sanctions imposed upon defendant Henry Roth and upon Louis H. Benjamin, Esq., each in the amount of $2,500; cross-motion otherwise denied.

Exercises

1. Go to the clerks' office of the Appellate Division and obtain a copy of an appellate brief.

2. Discuss how you would go about locating New York property owned by the obligor.

3. What is your opinion of the state sanctioning attorneys against initiating frivolous lawsuits? Explain.

4. What is the purpose of granting full faith and credit to judgments of sister states? Explain.

5. Go to the Appellate Term, Appellate Division, or Court of Appeals and attend an appellate hearing.

Exhibit

Notice of Motion to Appellate Division for Permission to Appeal to Court of Appeals or to Reargue Appeal

SUPREME COURT OF THE STATE OF NEW YORK
APPELLATE DIVISION: __________DEPARTMENT
PEOPLE OF THE STATE OF NEW YORK,
by ________________, Attorney General of
the State of New York

_______________ County
Index No.:
Petitioners-Respondents
-against-
Appellate Division
Docket No.:

______________, Inc. and ____________, Inc.

NOTICE OF MOTION

Respondents

____________ BANK

Respondent-Appellant

and ____________

Respondent

PLEASE TAKE NOTICE, that upon the annexed affirmation of ________________, Esq., dated _____________, 2000, and upon the Decision and Order of this Court dated _____________, 2000, which was entered in the above-entitled appeal and filed with the Clerk of the

Supreme Court of the State of New York, Appellate Division, Second Judicial Department on _____________, 2000, the undersigned will move this Court, at the Courthouse located at _________, New York, on the _____ day of ____________, 2000, at 9:30 in the forenoon or as soon thereafter as counsel can be heard to reargue the above-entitled appeal; or in the alternative, for an order pursuant to CPLR § 5602 for permission to appeal the aforesaid Decision and Order of this Court to the Court of Appeals; and, granting such other and further relief as the Court deems just and proper.

Please take notice that pursuant to CPLR§ 2214(b), answering affidavits, if any, are required to be served upon the undersigned at least seven (7) days before the return date of the motion.

Dated:

Yours, etc.

____
Attorney for Defendant

TO:

____
Attorney for Plaintiff
Address: _________________
Telephone Number: _________________

Chapter Eight

OTHER PROCEDURES

Introduction

The CPLR provides for special legal procedures that are available to parties with a legal conflict arising under specified circumstances. These procedures are commenced by filing a petition to show cause and a notice of petition (or order to show cause) with the clerk of the court where the proceeding will take place. The clerk can set a hearing date at the request of the moving party not less than eight days after service of the petition on the non-moving party. If the hearing date is set for eight days, the answer must be filed at least two days before the hearing; if the hearing date is set for more than 12 days after service, the answer must be filed at least seven days before to the hearing.

If there are no triable issues of fact, the court may make a summary disposition of the matter upon motion from either party. If there are triable issues of fact, the matter may be decided either by the court or by jury if a jury trial is permitted for that type of action. The parties, by motion, may make disclosure before the actual hearing, and the parties may make an "objection in point of law" in the answer or reply which acts as a form of motion to dismiss.

While all proceedings in the Surrogate's Court, which deals with decedents' estates, are deemed to be "special proceedings," the ordinary procedural rules previously discussed are applied. The other special proceedings that will be detailed in this chapter are proceedings permitted under Article 78 of the CPLR and arbitration proceedings pursuant to Article 75.

This chapter will also include a brief overview of the federal court system operating in New York, because not all New York litigation takes place in the state courts, and the federal courts have their own procedural rules.

Article 78 Proceedings

Types of Proceedings

Excluding Surrogate's Court proceedings, probably the most frequently encountered special proceedings are those proceedings detailed in Article 78. Three distinct types of actions are covered by Article 78.

1. Certiorari. Certiorari is a petition to review a decision arising from a quasi-judicial administrative action. The basis of the petition is that the petitioner contends the administrative determination was made without sufficient evidence to support the conclusion. In order to maintain a petition for certiorari there must actually have been an evidentiary hearing at the administrative level.

Example: *A zoning board has decided to disallow commercial enterprise in a particular area after one open hearing. A group of potential merchants petition for certiorari because they believe that the evidence presented at the board hearing indicated a community need for such commercial enterprises and the decision was made contrary to the evidence presented.*

2. Prohibition. A petition for prohibition is used to question whether a political body or officer is acting in excess of his or her jurisdiction; the petition seeks to restrain the unauthorized action. This type of proceeding may be maintained against a court:
   a. if there is a clear legal right
   b. when the court is acting without appropriate jurisdiction
   c. when directed to an inferior judicial tribunal.

Example: *The mayor of a city has unilaterally decided to end funding for a museum because of her disapproval of the museum's exhibits. The*

Board of Trustees of the museum may seek to petition for a writ of prohibition against the mayor to stop this action.

3. Mandamus. Mandamus is a procedure used to order a government or one of its subdivisions or officers to fulfill its legal obligation. Mandamus generally is used in three situations:
   a. when an agency fails to perform its function as required by law (procedural rather than substantive violations)
   b. there was procedural error in the agency's action
   c. the action taken was arbitrary and capricious.

Example: *Despite repeated efforts to have a housing authority inspect what tenants believe is an unsafe and unhealthy condition in a city-owned building, the housing authority has failed to act. The tenants' association may file a petition for mandamus to have the court order the housing authority to fulfill its legal requirement to make regular inspections of city-run facilities.*

Article 78 proceedings are not available in three situations:

1. An appeal procedure is available to the petitioner, but the appeal has not yet been taken.
2. The petitioner has a legal right to seek review of the complained of action.
3. The matter in question is a civil or criminal action.

The venue for Article 78 proceedings is the supreme court sitting in the county in which the action occurred, unless the action is against the county or the actions of the supreme court itself. Recall from Chapter One the Statute of Limitations for instituting an Article 78 proceedings is four months from the date of the injury, but the court has the discretion to apply laches if appropriate. **Laches** is an equitable doctrine permitting a court to expand or contract the period in which an action may be commenced. Article 78 proceedings are designed to provide relief against governmental action other than legislative action, but may also be used for quasi-legislative actions. Note that jury trials may be available at Article 78 proceedings if the party can demonstrate that the underlying claim is one that would normally be submitted to a jury for deliberation.

Procedure

An Article 78 proceeding begins with the filing of a Notice of Petition and a petition with the court. The petitioner must serve the respondent within 15 days of the expiration of the Statute of Limitations. The initial papers must be served at least 20 days before the hearing date, and the respondent's answer must be served at least five days prior to the hearing. If the petitioner wishes to respond to the answer, the petitioner's reply must be sent at least one day before the hearing. The supreme court hears petitions for prohibition and mandamus, whereas petitions for certiorari are determined by the Appellate Division. Article 78 proceedings may be stayed by motion of one of the parties or by the court on its own initiative.

The court may either grant or deny the motion, and restitution or damages are only permitted secondarily and only if the petitioner could have maintained a separate suit seeking such relief against the respondent (normally damages against the state are sought in the Court of Claims, but may be awarded pursuant to the Article 78 proceeding).

Arbitration

Under Article 75, arbitration awards are enforceable in court only if there is a written agreement between the parties to submit the matter to arbitration. CPLR § 7501. A party to an arbitration proceeding can challenge the arbitration on grounds of (CPLR § 7571):

1. the corruption, fraud, or misconduct of the arbitrator
2. the partiality of the arbitrator
3. the arbitrator exceeding his or her authority
4. the parties' failure to follow Article 75 procedures.

Any challenge to the arbitration award must be filed with the court within 90 days of the decision of the award.

Arbitration is a nonjudicial proceeding in which the parties select a person or a panel of persons to determine their rights and obligations. Attorneys commencing new actions in commercial, general, or matrimonial law are required to provide a **Notice of Dispute Resolution Alternatives** to their clients within 45 days of filing initial papers in order to inform the parties of alternative means of settling their dispute. The general rules of evidence do not apply to arbitration proceedings, and they may be held in a less formal setting than a court proceeding. Arbitration is favored in many instances because it is more expedient and less costly than the judicial process.

To initiate an arbitration proceeding, the party must file a notice of intention to arbitrate. If the other party objects to arbitration, he or she must file an objection to the notice within 20 days of the receipt of the notice. Also, a party may file a motion to stay the proceedings within 20 days of receipt of the notice pursuant to CPLR § 7503. Arbitration is precluded if

1. arbitration has not been agreed to in the written agreement between the parties unless they subsequently accede to arbitration
2. the agreement to arbitrate was induced by fraud
3. there is a condition precedent in the agreement prior to arbitration and that condition has not yet been met
4. the underlying contract between the parties is prohibited by law
5. the Statute of Limitations on the cause of action has expired
6. the matter is deemed res judicata.

If one of the parties is dilatory, the other party may make a motion with the court to compel arbitration. CPLR § 7503(a). A party to an arbitration proceeding may seek a provisional remedy of either attachment or preliminary injunction prior to the arbitration proceeding, and the court cannot review interlocutory relief granted by the arbitrator.

Example: The buyer and seller of lead piping have agreed to submit any controversy arising under the sales contract to arbitration with the arbitrator already named in the contract. There is a dispute regarding the quality of the piping delivered, and the seller serves the buyer with a notice to arbitrate. The buyer refuses to respond or appear at the scheduled hearing, and so the seller may make a motion to compel the buyer to submit to the arbitration to which he has previously agreed.

Federal Courts

Although this text is designed to discuss the procedures for maintaining civil suits in the state courts of New York, it is also necessary to provide a brief overview of the federal court system that operates within the state. Similar to the New York state court system, the federal courts provide a three-tiered court structure:

1. courts of original jurisdiction, known as the district courts. New York is divided into four federal districts.
2. intermediate courts of appeal, referred to as the circuit courts. New York is in the Second Circuit.
3. the United States Supreme Court, the court of last resort.

The federal courts have exclusive jurisdiction in the following matters:

- bankruptcy
- patent and copyright claims
- actions to which the United States is a party
- matters concerning foreign consuls and vice-consuls
- antitrust
- admiralty
- claims based on a federal statute
- postal matters
- matters involving the Internal Revenue Service
- national security and espionage.

The procedures for maintaining suits in the federal courts are governed by the Federal Rules of Civil Procedure; the CPLR has no application to matters in the federal court structure.

The jurisdiction of the federal courts is based on the following:

1. Federal Question. The matter in controversy is based on the United States Constitution, a treaty, or a federal statute, regardless of the amount in controversy.
2. Diversity of Citizenship. Diversity jurisdiction is based on the fact that *all* of the plaintiffs reside in different states than *all* of the defendants *and* the amount in controversy is greater than $75,000. Complete diversity is required for federal diversity jurisdiction; there is no diversity in claims between two non-permanent resident aliens.

If the court's jurisdiction is based on diversity and there is a substitution of parties after the action has commenced, the court's diversity jurisdiction is based on the original party to the action. If a party is impleaded there is no need for that party to meet the diversity requirement. If a partnership is a party, there must be diversity with all of the partners; if there is a class action, diversity is based on the residence of the named parties.

The amount in controversy must be greater than $75,000, and amounts can be aggregated to meet this amount.

When a federal court adjudicates a matter, it is required to follow the procedural rules enunciated in the Federal Rules of Civil Procedure, but must follow the substantive laws of the state in which the court is sitting if the basis of the jurisdiction is diversity, based on a Supreme Court case, *Erie R. v. Tompkins*, 304 U.S. 64 (1938).

Ethical Concerns

One of the ethical concerns that may arise with respect to instituting suits in a federal court is occasioned by a plaintiff leaving the jurisdiction just to create diversity so as to be able to access the diversity jurisdiction of the federal court, even though the plaintiff has no true intention of relinquishing New York residence or domicile. If this fraudulent relocation is discovered, the federal court is empowered to dismiss the suit.

Chapter Review

The CPLR permits two types of special proceedings to provide relief in a more efficient manner than a full trial. The first is contained in Article 78 which permits citizens to seek an order against the state executive and judicial branches of government. The citizen may petition for certiorari for the court to review actions of administrative bodies, for prohibition to compel a government official to stop a particular action, or for mandamus to have the court compel a government official to fulfill a legal obligation. Article 78 proceedings must be brought within four months of the alleged injury to allow for a quick resolution of the matter.

The CPLR also provides procedures for arbitration in which the parties, by contractual agreement, specify that controversies will be decided outside of the court system by persons chosen by the parties to resolve their dispute. The CPLR procedures are in effect to ensure that the arbitrator follows appropriate procedures and remains fair and impartial to the parties. Arbitration is a quick and cost effective method of resolving disputes.

In addition to the New York state court system, litigants also have access to the federal court system in New York if the matter in controversy involves a federal question or there is complete diversity of citizenship and the amount in controversy exceeds $75,000. The purpose of the federal court's diversity jurisdiction is to allow an out-of-state resident an impartial forum in which to present his or her cause of action against an in-state resident.

Key Terms

Arbitration – method of resolving disputes by using an independent person to resolve disputes outside of the court process

Article 78 proceedings – special proceedings for certiorari, prohibition, and mandamus

Certiorari – judicial review of administrative actions

Diversity jurisdiction – one method of invoking the jurisdiction of the federal courts

Federal Rules of Civil Procedure – rules governing procedure in the federal courts

Laches – equitable period in which to institute a suit

Mandamus – order to compel a governmental official to fulfill a legal obligation

Notice of Dispute Resolution Alternatives – notice given to parties in commercial, general or matrimonial actions to alert them to non-judicial methods of resolving their disputes

Prohibition – order to compel a government official to stop actions that exceed his or her authority

Edited Judicial Decisions

New York City Health and Hospitals Corporation v. McBarnette
84 NY2D 194 (1994)

This appeal raises the question we left open in *New York State Assn. of Counties v. Axelrod* (78 NY2d 158, 166) (NYSAC): what Statute of Limitations should be applied to declaratory judgment actions brought to challenge promulgated Medicaid reimbursement rates on the ground that they are irrational or affected with error of law. Reaffirming the principles that were articulated in such cases as *Solnick v. Whalen* (49 NY2d 224), we hold that in the circumstances presented here the four-month Statute of Limitations for proceedings against a body or officer is applicable (*see*, CPLR § 217).

Plaintiff, which operates both hospitals and residential care facilities, commenced this declaratory judgment action to challenge two separate aspects of its Medicaid reimbursement rate. The first part of plaintiff's challenge sought relief from defendants' effort to use a "recalibration adjustment" that was promulgated in December 1991 to calculate its residential-care facility rates for the rate years between 1989 and 1991 (10 NYCRR 86-2.31 [a]). The proper resolution of this issue is governed by *Matter of Jewish Home & Infirmary v. Commissioner of N.Y. State Dept. of Health* (84 NY2d 252 [decided herewith]), in which we hold that Public Health Law § 2807(7)(a) prohibits such retroactive rate-making.

The second part of plaintiff's challenge involves a disputed change in the manner in which hospitals are reimbursed for services provided to certain of their patients. Effective January 1, 1988, defendants replaced their existing per-diem method of computing reimbursement with a new per-case approach. Services for patients whose hospital stays "straddled" the period before and after the new system's effective date were initially to be reimbursed under the former per-diem computation method. However, by letter dated July 3, 1989, the Commissioner of Social Services, after consultation with the Department of Health (DOH) and the Division of the Budget, advised hospitals providing service to Medicaid recipients that only those "straddle" patients categorized as needing "acute" care would be subject to the apparently more favorable per-diem rate. Services to "alternative level of care" patients, (i.e., those who could be cared for in residential nursing facilities), would be reimbursed on the newer per-case basis. Reimbursement amounts in excess of the allowable rates that had already been paid were to be recouped through reductions in current payments.

The July 3, 1989, rate decision was challenged in a timely CPLR Article 78 proceeding brought by the Hospital Association of New York State (*Matter of Hospital Assn. v. Axelrod,* 165 AD2d 152 [Feb. 14, 1991], *lv. denied*, 78 NY2d 853) (HANYS). Although it was aware of the HANYS litigation, plaintiff, which is not a member of the Hospital Association, decided not to intervene or commence a separate suit, choosing instead to rely on that organization's efforts to obtain relief.

The Appellate Division held in HANYS that the statute governing reimbursement for "straddle patients" did not leave room for distinguishing between "acute care" patients and "alternative level of care" patients. Accordingly, the policy was deemed arbitrary and *unlawful* (165 AD2d, at 154–155). As a result of that decision, defendants, who represent agencies responsible for administering the Medicaid program, were ordered to repay to the Hospital Association and its members any funds that had been withheld or recouped pursuant to the invalidated decision.

In October of 1991, plaintiff applied for a refund of moneys that defendants had recouped pursuant to the rule invalidated in HANYS. After it was advised that defendants did not intend to grant such a refund, plaintiff promptly brought the present proceeding in February 1992 to challenge both the July 3, 1989, rule and the more recent refusal of its refund request.

On cross motions for summary judgment, the Supreme Court ordered defendants to recalculate plaintiff's nursing home reimbursement rate without regard to the "recalibration adjustment." With respect to the claims that were based upon the invalidated "straddle patient" rate determination, Supreme Court concluded that the four-month Statute of Limitations for CPLR Article 78 proceedings was applicable and that, accordingly, those claims were time-barred.

On plaintiff's appeal, the Appellate Division affirmed the first aspect of Supreme Court's ruling, but reversed on the latter point. Holding that the action was, in reality, one for reimbursement under title XIX of the Social Security Act (42 USC § 1396 et seq.), the Appellate Division cited the Second Circuit's decision in *Hollander v. Brezenoff* (787 F2d 834), applied the three-year limitations period for actions to recover on a liability imposed by statute (CPLR § 214[2]) and ruled the action timely. Inasmuch as the merits had previously been resolved in *HANYS (supra),* the Court granted plaintiff summary judgment on its claim for a refund. This appeal, taken by permission of this Court, ensued.

Initially, we note that the Appellate Division's reliance on *Hollander v. Brezenoff (supra)* was misplaced. The only issue in Hollander was whether a proceeding to enforce a social service agency's obligation to pay a Medicaid provider was governed by the six-year limitations period for actions on a contractual obligation (CPLR § 213 [2]) or was instead governed by the three-year period for actions on a liability imposed by statute (CPLR § 214 [2]). The court was not called upon to consider whether the shorter four-month limitations for proceedings against a body or officer (CPLR § 217) was applicable. Consequently, its holding has no persuasive significance here.

The proper starting point for determining which Statute of Limitations should be applied in a proceeding or action against a State or municipal governmental entity is this Court's 1980 decision in *Solnick v. Whalen* (49 NY2d 224 *supra*). In that case, the Court held that when the proceeding has been commenced in the form of a declaratory judgment action, for which no specific Statute of Limitations is prescribed, "it is necessary to examine the substance of that action to identify the relationship out of which the claim arises and the relief sought" in order to resolve which Statute of Limitations is *applicable (49 NY2d, at 229; cf., Koerner v. State of New York*, 62 NY2d 442, 447 [Solnick rule does not govern when "a specific limitations period is clearly applicable to a given action, (and) there is no need to ascertain whether another form of proceeding is available"]). Only if there is no other "form of proceeding for which a specific limitation period is statutorily provided" may the six-year catch-all limitations period provided in CPLR § 213(1) be invoked (49 NY2d, at 229–230). In other words, if the claim could have been made in a form other than an action for a declaratory judgment and the limitations period for an action in that form has already expired, the time for asserting the claim cannot be extended through the simple expedient of denominating the action one for declaratory relief (49 NY2d, at 230; *accord, Press v. County of Monroe*, 50 NY2d 695, 701). Of course, when the claim is one against a governmental body or officer, the form of action that immediately springs to mind is a proceeding brought under CPLR Article 78, a traditional, and surely the most common, vehicle for challenging a governmental decision or action.

Plaintiff contends that an article 78 proceeding is inapplicable here because the challenged agency decision is legislative in nature in that it applies across the board to all hospitals providing care to "straddle patients." In support of this position, plaintiff cites a line of cases holding that article 78 does not lie to challenge a legislative act (*e.g., Bryant Ave. Tenants' Assn. v. Koch*, 71 NY2d 856; *Matter of DuBois v. Town Bd.*, 35 NY2d 617; *Matter of Kovarsky v. Housing & Dev. Admin.*, 31 NY2d 184; *Matter of Overhill Bldg. Co. v. Delany*, 28 NY2d 449). However, despite the unquestionable validity of this line of cases, we conclude that further analysis is necessary because there remains some confusion as to what constitutes a "legislative act" *(cf., Press v. County of Monroe, supra*, at 703-704, with *id.*, at 704–706 [Jasen, J., dissenting], and *Solnick v. Whalen, supra, at 231;* see, 8 Weinstein-Korn-Miller, N.Y. Civ. Prac. P. 7801.02, at 78-11), and, consequently, the formula on which plaintiff relies is insufficient to resolve the issue presented by plaintiff's case.

Among the apparent sources of the confusion is *Matter of Lakeland Water Dist. v. Onondaga County Water Auth.* (24 NY2d 400), in which the Court held that article 78 was unavailable to challenge a rate decision made by a public benefit corporation charged with the responsibility of regulating the price of water to private customers and water districts. Drawing on the principle that an article 78 proceeding may not be used to review legislative action, the Lakeland Court reasoned that "an order of an administrative agency fixing rates is deemed a legislative act, at least where no provision has been made for notice and a hearing" (*id.*, at 407). Inasmuch as the rate determination at issue was not subject to any notice and hearing requirements, the Court concluded, it was legislative in nature and not subject to article 78 review (24 NY2d, at 409).

Lakeland was followed by *Solnick v. Whalen (supra*, at 231–232, and n. 3), in which this Court, in an effort to explain that decision, suggested that an agency rate-setting determination may be "legislative" or "administrative" depending upon whether it is an "across-the-board" ruling or is instead determinative only of an "individualized rate[ ] established for a particular litigant". However, in *Press v. County of Monroe (supra),* a case involving a generally applicable rate schedule, the Court simply relegated the analysis in Lakeland to a "cf." citation and did not follow, or even discuss, the Solnick distinction. Instead, it referred to an entirely different principle (i.e., that article 78 is not the proper vehicle for challenging the constitutionality of a legislative enactment) (*see, e.g., Matter of Ames Volkswagen v. State Tax Commn.*, 47 NY2d 345, 348; *New York Pub. Interest Research Group v. Steingut*, 40 NY2d 250, 254; *Matter of Merced v. Fisher*, 38 NY2d 557, 559) and then went on to hold that the rate-setting decision at issue was not "legislative" because it lacked a number of traits that ordinarily characterize enactments of a legislative body (50 NY2d, at 701–704). Despite Press, subsequent cases involving rate setting and other types of governmental determinations have relied on the Solnick distinction between generalized and individualized decision-making (*see, e.g., Matter of Klein v. Axelrod*, 54 NY2d 818, *aff'g.* 81 AD2d 935*; cf.*, *Eve v. Power Auth.*, 123 AD2d 532 [relying on Lakeland distinction premised on notice and hearing requirements]; *but cf., Lenihan v. City of New York*, 85 AD2d 562, *aff'd.* 58 NY2d 679).

Viewed in the proper light, the difficulty in this field seems to lie not in the rationales or results of the salient cases, but rather in the ambiguity of the terminology and the absence of a cohesive analytical structure to lend perspective to the existing case law. The case law often does not distinguish between true legislative acts and those administrative acts that are deemed "quasi-legislative," and there has been little reasoned discussion as to why the latter class of acts should necessarily be treated in the same way as the former. Moreover, while it may be helpful to consider the distinctions drawn in Lakeland and Solnick between generalized and individualized decision-making and the existence or nonexistence of a notice-and-hearing requirement, these categories cannot adequately be understood in the legal and historical vacuum in which they are often discussed.

The maxim that article 78 does not lie to challenge legislative acts is derived from the separation-of-powers doctrine which made the use of the judiciary's "prerogative writ" unavailable as a vehicle for challenging an act of a legislative body (*e.g., Matter of Neddo v. Schrade*, 270 NY 97; *Matter of Long Is. R. R. Co. v. Hylan*, 240 NY 199; *People ex rel. Trustees of Vil. of Jamaica v. Board of Supervisors*, 131 NY 468; *see*, McLaughlin, *Practice Commentaries, McKinney's Consol. Laws of N.Y.*, Book 7B, CPLR § C7801:1, at 25 [1981]). That same principle, however, has no application to the quasi-legislative acts of administrative agencies. With respect to those acts, there is no reason why article 78 review in the nature of "mandamus to review" should not be available to the extent that the challenge fits within the language and accompanying gloss of CPLR §§ 7801 and 7803(3).

CPLR § 7801 provides that the relief historically available by the former writs of certiorari to review, mandamus and prohibition are all available now through proceedings brought under article 78. CPLR § 7803 supplements that provision by setting forth "[t]he only questions that may be raised in a proceeding under ... article [78]." Taken together, these statutes and the body of common law they incorporate are necessarily the prime reference points for determining whether a particular claim against a public body or officer may be brought in the form of an article 78 proceeding. Thus, where a quasi-legislative act by an administrative agency such as a rate determination is challenged on the ground that it "was made in violation of lawful procedure, was affected by an error of law or was arbitrary and capricious or an abuse of discretion" (CPLR § 7803[3]), a proceeding in the form prescribed by article 78 can be maintained and, as a corollary matter, the four-month Statute of Limitations that ordinarily governs such proceedings is applicable.

To be sure, in most situations, agencies' generally applicable decisions do not lend themselves to consideration on their merits under the provisions for mandamus to review, because they concern rational choices among competing policy considerations and are thus not amenable to analysis under the "arbitrary and capricious" standard. Nonetheless, there are certainly cases in which even a nonindividualized, generally applicable quasi-legislative act such as a regulation or an across-the-board rate-computation ruling can be challenged as being "affected by an error of law," "arbitrary and capricious" or lacking a rational basis (CPLR § 7803[3]). The claim raised by plaintiff here presents precisely such a case.

As did the petitioners in HANYS, plaintiff here is claiming that defendants' decision concerning the proper method for computing the reimbursement rate for "straddle patients" was unlawful and arbitrary and capricious in that it had no foundation in the relevant statutes (*see*, *HANYS*, 165 AD2d, at 154–156, *supra*). The nature of plaintiff's claim requires it to convince the court that defendants promulgated a rule affecting hospital rates that represented an irrational construction of the governing statutes. Such a claim is plainly encompassed within the grounds for mandamus to review set forth in CPLR § 7803(3), which include "whether a determination ... was affected by an error of law or was arbitrary and capricious" (see also, NYSAC, supra [claim that rate adjustment regulation was arbitrary because it was not based on empirical facts]). Additionally, since the claim concerns a quasi-legislative act of an administrative agency rather than a true legislative enactment, there is no sound basis for invoking the historical bar precluding use of the prerogative writ as a vehicle for reviewing true legislative acts, even though the regulation in question is indisputably one of general applicability. Accordingly, plaintiff's challenge could have been brought in the form of an article 78 proceeding, and the present action, brought more than 2 1/2 years after the July 3, 1989, letter advising of defendants' policy was sent, was untimely.

We note that our holding with regard to the Statute of Limitations question presented here is in accord with the public policies identified in *Solnick v. Whalen* (*supra*, at 232) and reiterated in *Press v. County of Monroe* (*supra*, at 704). A rule that requires those subject to regulatory decisions such as Medicaid rate-making to bring their challenges promptly facilitates rational planning by all concerned parties and ensure "that the operation of government [will] not be trammeled by stale litigation and stale determinations" (*Solnick v. Whalen, supra,* at 232, *quoting Mundy v. Nassau County Civ. Serv. Commn.*, 44 NY2d 352, 359 [Breitel, Ch. J., dissenting]).

We are not persuaded by plaintiff's opposing contention that the policies represented by the decision in *Matter of Jones v. Berman* (37 NY2d 42) militate against such a rule because it compels all potentially aggrieved litigants to bring duplicative suits rather than waiting to see what the outcome will be in a pending test case. In Jones, the Court held only that a class action is generally an inappropriate vehicle for asserting a claim against a governmental entity, since "where governmental operations are involved" similarly situated parties other than the individual litigant "will be adequately protected under the principles of *stare decisis*" (37 NY2d, at 57; *accord, Matter of Rivera v. Trimarco*, 36 NY2d 747, 749). By its terms, that holding concerns itself only with the inefficiency of using the class action form when the prospective rights of interested nonlitigants can be safeguarded by other means. Nothing in the Jones decision suggests that the same policies justify either the use of a long limitations period or the creation of a toll solely to enable aggrieved parties to sit on their existing rights pending the outcome of an early challenge brought by others (*cf., American Pipe & Constr. Co. v. Utah*, 414 US 538, 554).

Finally, inasmuch as plaintiff had lost the right to challenge the validity of the underlying rate decision through its own inaction, it had no legal basis for its October 1991 post-HANYS demand for a refund of the moneys that had been recouped pursuant to the recently invalidated "straddle patient" policy. Thus, to the extent that plaintiff's complaint asserted a timely cause of action based on the refusal of that demand, the claim was lacking in substantive merit and was properly rejected. We decline to adopt plaintiff's contention that equal protection principles guarantee it the same relief as was afforded to the members of the Hospital Association of New York, all of whom received refunds after the HANYS decision was handed down. Since the Hospital Association was a party in HANYS and had standing to represent its members, defendants could rationally distinguish between those members, whose rights had been adjudicated in HANYS, and plaintiff, a nonparty whose rights had not been addressed in that or any other judicial proceeding. Plaintiff's argument that its property was taken without just compensation is equally meritless, as is its contention that the HANYS judgment itself required that defendants give refunds to all affected hospitals. A plain reading of that judgment demonstrates that it granted relief only to the petitioners in the HANYS proceeding and to the represented member hospitals.

Accordingly, the order of the Appellate Division should be modified, without costs, by reinstating the judgment of the Supreme Court and, as modified, affirmed.

In the Matter of Gershen
163 AD2d 17 (1990)

Order and judgment (one paper), Supreme Court, New York County (Irma Vidal Santaella, J.), entered on or about December 5, 1989, which granted the petition of petitioners to stay arbitration and denied respondents' cross motion to consolidate this arbitration proceeding with another pending arbitration proceeding, unanimously reversed, on the law, the facts and in the exercise of discretion, the petition to stay arbitration is dismissed and the cross motion to consolidate the two pending arbitrations is granted, with costs.

From 1964 to 1987, petitioners William R. Gershen and George J. Gershen (the Gershens) were shareholders of Halo Fashions, Inc., a firm engaged in the manufacture and sale of garments, with respondents Werner and Gunther Hess (the Hesses). Pursuant to an agreement which became effective July 1, 1987, the Gershens sold their shares of Halo to the company and to Charles Bezner. As a result, Bezner and each of the Hesses became one-third shareholders of Halo. Paragraph 8 of the contract of sale contained a broad arbitration clause. On July 1, 1987, Bezner and the Hesses also entered into a stockholders' agreement with Halo which contained the identical arbitration provisions. By separate agreement dated January 1, 1988, Bezner became a 50 percent shareholder of Halo with the Hesses retaining a 50 percent interest.

Bezner thereafter commenced an arbitration proceeding before the American Arbitration Association against the Hesses and Halo alleging corporate mismanagement and breach of fiduciary obligations. The Hesses and Halo then commenced a separate arbitration proceeding against the Gershens seeking indemnification from all claims sustained against them in the proceeding initiated by Bezner.

After the Gershens moved to stay the arbitration commenced by the Hesses and Halo, the Hesses cross-moved for consolidation of the arbitration with the Bezner arbitration. The Supreme Court granted the petition to stay the arbitration on the ground that the arbitration against the Gershens was premature since a prime obligation of the Hesses had not yet been established and since the Gershens' liability could not be ascertained prior to a determination in the Bezner arbitration. The court also denied the cross motion to consolidate.

The Supreme Court erred in granting the petition staying arbitration since it was undisputed that a valid agreement was entered into by the parties, the agreement was complied with and since the claim was not barred by the applicable Statute of Limitations (CPLR § 7502[b]; *Matter of United Nations Dev. Corp. v. Norkin Plumbing Co.*, 45 NY2d 358). Although the Gershens contend that it is premature to require the arbitration of the indemnification or contribution claims, once the court determines that a dispute within the scope of the arbitration clause exists, "the court shall not consider whether the claim with respect to which arbitration is sought is tenable, or otherwise pass upon the merits of the dispute" (CPLR § 7501; *and see, Matter of Cowper Co. [Hires-Turner Glass Co.]*, 51 NY2d 937; *Bellevue S. Assocs. v. Heckler Elec. Co.*, 95 AD2d 721, 723, *aff'd* 62 NY2d 873). The agreements' broad arbitration clauses contain no condition precedent to the arbitration of the instant dispute and the issues may best be determined by the arbitrators on the basis of their interpretation of the contracts (*supra*).

The Supreme Court also erred in granting George Gershen's petition to stay arbitration since he failed to apply to stay the proceedings within 20 days after service upon him of the notice to arbitrate (CPLR § 7503[c]; *Aetna Life & Cas. Co. v. Stekardis*, 34 NY2d 182; *Matter of Allstate Ins. Co. [Jones-Barnett]*, 143 AD2d 570).

We further find that it was an improvident exercise of discretion for the Supreme Court to have denied the cross motion to consolidate the arbitration proceedings in light of the existence of at least one common party, common issues, the possibility of inconsistent judgments should separate proceedings be conducted and since the Gershens have failed to demonstrate that they would be prejudiced by such consolidation (*Matter of Cowper Co. [Hires-Turner Glass Co.], supra; County of Sullivan v. Edward L. Nezelek, Inc.*, 42 NY2d 123; *Matter of Vigo S. S. Corp. [Marship Corp.*], 26 NY2d 157, cert. denied sub. nom. *Snare Corp. v. Vigo S. S. Corp.*, 400 U.S. 819).

Exercises

1. Obtain a copy of the Federal Rules of Civil Procedure and compare its provisions to the CPLR.

2. Why do you think the Statute of Limitations for Article 78 proceedings is so short? Explain.

3. Indicate some potential benefits and detriments of the arbitration process.

4. Compare and contrast prohibition and mandamus.

5. Why do you think petitions for certiorari are determined by the Appellate Division? Explain.

TIME LIMITS

Pleading	Time in Days
Affidavit of Service on Out-of-State Defendant	30 days
Filing Process as Result of *Ex Parte* Order	5 days
Service After Order of Provisional Remedy for Statute of Limitations	30 days
Service After Order of Attachment	60 days (120 days if granted extension)
Filing Notice of Claim for Attachment for Malpractice After Ten Years	90 days after instituting action
Tolling of Statute of Limitations by Service of Process	60 days provided defendant served after filing
Notice of Claim	90 days before filing suit
Service of Summons after expiration of Statute of Limitations on 4-Month Statute	120 or 15 days
Leave and Mail Service	20 days after delivery
Filing Proof of Service	20 days after leaving or mailing; service complete 10 days after filing
Return Receipt by Defendant	30 days
Defendant's Appearance	20 days after personal service; 30 days after substituted service; 20 days after sending receipt
Serving Complaint on Defendant	20 days after request
Defendant's Answer or Motion	20 days after receipt of complaint
Notice of Dispute Resolution Alternatives	45 days after filing suit
Motion to Dismiss for Insufficient Service	60 days after service or answer
Answer to Demand for Change of Venue	5 days
Motion to Change Venue	15 days
To Approve Class Action	60 days

Pleading	Time in Days
Service on 3d Party	120 days after filing 3d party summons and complaint
3d Party Answer	20 days after service
Amending Complaint After 3d Party Complaint Without Leave of Court	20 days after service on plaintiff
Default Against Incompetent	20 days after appointment of representative
Response to Bill of Particulars	30 days after service of demand
Supplement Bill of Particulars	30 days before trial without leave of court
Start Discovery	7 days after answer to Bill of Particulars
Answer to Interrogatories	5 days added if sent by ordinary mail; 1 day added if sent by overnight mail
Service of Notice of Motion	8 days before hearing; 9 days if overnight mail used
Response to Motion	2 days before response date; 7 days if hearing is 12-17 days after service
Reply to Response to Motion	1 before hearing
Amend Pleading Without Motion	20 days
Motion for Summary Judgment	Anytime after answer, but no later than 120 after notice of issue
Hearing on Summary Judgment Motion	20 days after personal service; 30 days after substituted service
Response to Summary Judgment Motion	10 days prior to hearing
Service of Summons After Order of Attachment	60 days
Motion to Confirm	5 days
Service of Notice of Lis Pendens	30 days after filing
Notice to Confirm (Attachment & Replevin)	5 days
Motion to Reclaim Replevied Property	10 days after service
Motion of Default	Leave of Court
Notice to Defaulting Party	5 days if any appearance made; 20 days for nonpayment of contract obligation

Pleading	Time in Days
Motion for Relief of Default Judgment	1 year
Notice of Deposition	20 days before deposition; 25 days if mailed
Cross Notice of Deposition	10 days before deposition; 15 days if mailed
Notice of Deposition of Non-Party	20 days (subpoena required)
Response to Written Interrogatories	20 days
Request for Inspection of Documents and Physical Evidence	20 days before inspection
Response to Demand for Admissions	20 days
Objection to Discovery	20 days of service
File Notice of Issue	40 days after service of summons
File for Medical Malpractice Preference	60 days after service of summons
Notice of Appeal	30 days after entry of judgment
File Cross Appeal	10 days after service or 30 days after entry of notice, whichever is longer
Stay of Execution	valid for 5 days after appellate ruling or notice of appeal denied
Execution and Levy of Judgment	60 days after order
File Notice of Execution	30 days after judgment or appeal
Execution of Judgment	30 days after proof of service
Service of Foreign Judgment Order	30 days after filing in N.Y.
Execution on Foreign Judgment	30 days after proof of service
Hearing Date for Special Proceedings	8 days after service
Answer to Motion for Special Proceeding	2 days if hearing is within 8 days; 7 days if hearing is within 12 days
Challenge to Arbitration	90 days after filing
Objection to Notice to Arbitrate	20 days after receipt
Motion to Stay Arbitration	20 days after notice

INDEX

A

B

C

D

N

O

P

Q

R

S

T